Unleashing
Your Creativity
After 50!

By Gene Perret

Quill
Driver
Books

Sanger, California

Printed in the United States of America.

Published by
Quill Driver Books/Word Dancer Press, Inc.
1254 Commerce Way, Sanger, CA 93657
559-876-2170 / 800-497-4909
QuillDriverBooks.com

Quill Driver Books/Word Dancer Press books may be purchased for educational, fund-raising, business or promotional use. Please contact Special Markets, Quill Driver Books/Word Dancer Press, Inc. at the above address or phone numbers.

Quill Driver Books/Word Dancer Press Project Cadre:
Doris Hall, Christine Hernandez, David Marion,
Stephen Blake Mettee, Cassandra Williams
First Printing

ISBN 1-884956-73-4 • 978-1884956-73-7

**To order a copy of this book, please call
1-800-497-4909.**

Library of Congress Cataloging-in-Publication Data
Perret, Gene.
Unleashing your creativity after 50! / by Gene Perret.
p. cm.
Includes index.
ISBN-13: 978-1-884956-81-2 (pbk.)
ISBN-10: 1-884956-81-5 (pbk.)
1. Middle-aged persons—Life skills guides. 2. Middle age—
Psychological aspects. 3. Creative ability. 4. Creative ability in
old age. I. Title.
HQ1059.4.P48 2008
153.3'50844—dc22

2007050578

to
Phyllis Diller

Whose sense of humor
and enthusiasm
are an inspiration
to all who come into contact
with her

Contents

Foreword

For decades, Gene Perret has made people laugh, yet not many of us outside show business know who he is. That's because Gene writes the jokes other people tell, people like Bob Hope and Phyllis Diller and Carol Burnett.

But for the last decade or so, Gene has concentrated on writing his own funny material, and it's being published in book after book and magazine after magazine. I know because I was his editor at *Arizona Highways* magazine for more than ten years.

His monthly column called "Wit Stop" drew an enormous following. I have edited magazine and newspaper columnists for most of my adult life and there is no doubt Gene's column was the most popular—not just by a little, but by far.

So when Gene speaks of creativity, I listen, and so should everyone else.

In fact, years ago I listened so intently to Gene that I took up a secondary profession. I teach humor writing at Arizona State University West. Here's how it came about:

I attended a Gene Perret Round Table humor workshop. Mainly, I was curious about how sitcom writers and stand-up comedians did what they did. I was not prepared for what happened.

The other attendees were all professionals who were used to performing. The first morning as we were having coffee, Gene invited each person to introduce herself or himself. As each person stood up, a comedy routine followed. They were performing! I, of course, panicked and tried to think of something funny.

When it came my turn I stood up, recited my name, mentioned I edited a magazine and said, "In this group I feel like Dan Quayle at a party for grownups." To my surprise everyone laughed and I sat down. That was the most success I had for the rest of the workshop.

But I was motivated to learn as much as I could about comedy writing. I attended other Gene Perret workshops, watched him teach a comedy seminar at Northern Arizona University, and read all his books, some several times. I learned.

Gene motivated me and he'll motivate you to be creative. His attitude—clearly evident in his books—is always optimistic, always positive. And, that I-can-do-it attitude is contagious.

Everyone has talent, but often that talent is underutilized. The family, the job, the fast-paced culture we live in, and a myriad of other concerns often keep us from developing our latent talents. Sometimes we don't even realize we have those hidden talents.

In the writing class I teach, I tell the students the first third of the class will be devoted to joke writing. It never fails to draw a chorus of groans as students protest they have no talent for humor writing.

I promise them by the second class they will be telling jokes that evoke laughter. And by the second class there is so much laughter that students in nearby classrooms wonder what is going on.

So if you think you are not creative, if you believe you possess no hidden talents to stimulate, pay attention to Gene Perret. You will be surprised at what you discover.

Bob Early
Arizona Highways magazine editor, retired

Chapter 1

Life Happens

John Lennon once said, "Life is what happens to you while you're busy making other plans." All of us as youngsters had dreams, aspirations, fantasies, goals, and we unconsciously planned a pie-in-the-sky future for ourselves. A few of our dreams may have been bizarre, unreasonable, and perhaps unattainable, but they were there—real at the time. Some of us wanted to be ballerinas, others airline pilots. Many wanted to be great artists or actors in the movies. Even though the Wild West was gone and the frontiers were mostly conquered, some of us still wanted to be Indian scouts. Me? I wanted to be a cowboy hero like Gene Autry or Roy Rogers. I also wanted to be a football star, baseball star, and basketball star. Often I dreamed of teaming with a school chum to form a world-famous comedy team like Abbott and Costello or Martin and Lewis.

Idolized pop singer was also in my catalogue of intentions. As a first or second grader, I would sit on the step in front of my house singing softly to myself—in fact, barely audibly. Still I would fantasize that some record producer in my town would stroll by, hear my soothing Crosby-like voice, and jump up and down excitedly, knowing that he had discovered the next entertainment sensation.

None of them did.

Life happened. All the record producers in my town, if there were any, must have strolled down some other street.

Be honest, you had naïve ambitions, too, probably with plans for their fulfillment that were at least as ridiculous as mine. But then Life *happened.*

Once reality intrudes, it's hard to banish. Practicality is quite persuasive. It can convince us that we have to make a living, that we don't have the skills or the talent, that we owe something to our parents, or that we might make fools of ourselves in this silly pursuit. Reality uses any argument it can to steer us in the practical, traditional direction.

That's not necessarily a bad thing. Honestly, many of our childish fantasies should have been discarded. Also, many of you have had rewarding and happy journeys along the practical and traditional paths where Life led you. Very few doctors are kicking themselves today because they didn't become singing cowboys. Many mothers are happy with their husbands and proud of their children and wouldn't trade them in for a ballet career.

For some, the traditional, practical vocation was their childhood dream. One day in our fourth grade class, the teacher polled the students, asking what each wanted to be in life and why. One classmate told of a next-door neighbor playmate of his—a young girl who had died of cancer. He was so saddened by this loss that he vowed to one day become a doctor in order to help, and perhaps save, those who were sick.

He did become a doctor and practiced in the neighborhood where we grew up. Today he is an administrator in a hospital in that area.

It's interesting that I don't remember what I said in response to that teacher's query. In fact, I don't remember what any of my other classmates said. But this lad's response was so motivated and so impassioned that I've remembered it to this day.

Some of you readers, too, may have outfoxed Life at its own game.

Life, though, usually adjusts very quickly. When it comes to a fork in the road, it can yank us along the path it decides on rather than the path we may choose. It reminds me of the mobster in an old show business joke:

This gangster was very menacing and powerful. He went to a local nightclub owner and said, "My nephew wants to be a singer. This kid is good. He's better than Sinatra, better than Tony Bennett, better than all of them. He's my sister's kid and I want you to book him into the club and get the biggest talent agent in the world to come and see him."

The club owner said, "Gee, I can't get the head of William Morris to come to my small club. He's a busy man. He has other things to do."

The mobster said threateningly, "Get him here."
The club owner did.

The young man sang for the famous talent agent. After his performance, the menacing gangster asked the theatrical agent, "What do you think?"

The agent said honestly, "Look, I make my living booking the best entertainers in the world—singers, dancers, actors. This kid is terrible and I can't handle him."

The hood thought for a bit and then said, "That's OK. I'll make him a boxer."

That's the way Life can nudge us along paths we never considered. Some of you may have been led along paths you never considered. Later, many discovered that it wasn't a bad route. They found satisfaction, happiness, and even wealth in the alternative that Life selected for them.

Others stayed with their childhood dreams. From the time Tiger Woods was a toddler he desired to become a professional golfer, and he focused on the game. He still does today—with very satisfying results. My buddy who vowed to become a doctor stayed with his decision. It prompted him to study hard and keep his grades high enough to be accepted into medical school, to earn his degree, to persevere through his internship, and eventually to hang his shingle in the "old neighborhood."

Regardless of which of the above categories you fit into, though, surely some childish desires remain alive inside you. It may be one;

they may be many. Sure, wanting to grow up to be a cowboy may have been childish, but there are dude ranches all over the country catering to that childhood dream. Those of us who didn't make it as big-league baseball players still might take a well-earned vacation to a baseball fantasy camp. Young ladies may have abandoned their goal of playing the lead in a professional production of *Swan Lake*, but it's possible that their new goal will be to convince their husbands to attend an Arthur Murray dance studio where together they can learn some fancy and flashy steps to the waltz or the tango.

As John Lennon observed, we've all lived our lives while we were busy making other plans, but many of our childhood fancies have not been completely snuffed out.

Even success or achievement doesn't eliminate some of those early desires. I once worked on a Bob Hope television special in Tahiti. Between tapings, I asked if I could borrow the guitar of one of the musicians. I began picking out a few tunes on the instrument. I'm not a musician by any means and I know very little about music, but I can improvise passably on a guitar. As I plucked away, Bob Hope, who was watching, said, "I'd give anything to be able to do that."

Hope seemingly had everything—fame, fortune, respect—but he would have enjoyed being able to play a musical instrument.

Another Bob Hope tale illustrates this same point. Hope had a friend who was a very successful, wealthy businessman. As they chatted one day, this friend told Bob Hope that he always wanted to know how to tap dance. He asked the comedian to give him a few lessons. Hope taught him a simple dance routine. The businessman practiced diligently and in several charity shows he performed the vaudeville dance routine on stage with Hope. Again, he had everything one could wish for, but he wanted to learn to tap dance.

Childhood desires don't die; they just hide.

I cite these two examples because there is a big difference between them. The first goal remained unfulfilled. Bob Hope never did learn how to play a musical instrument. Of course, he was busy doing other things. Someone once asked him what he would do differently if he had his life to live over again. He replied, "If I had my life to live over again, I don't think I'd have the time." So for him, the desire to play a musical instrument remained a desire.

His friend, though, wanted to learn to tap dance, so he did. I'm sure he didn't threaten Fred Astaire, but he did learn a few steps and performed a routine.

All of us have some unfulfilled wishes and now that we've gotten our forty-ninth year behind us, it's a good time to start revisiting a few of them. That's what this book is about—encouraging you to unleash some of the creativity you may have been suppressing.

Before we get to that, though, it may be helpful to consider why some of these dreams were abandoned in the first place. We'll discuss this in the following chapter.

Chapter 2

That Was Then . . .

Where did those dreams we were once so passionate about go? What happened to them? There are many possible reasons why they were shunted aside, hidden, abandoned, or simply forgotten about.

1. Adults Discouraged Us:

Well-meaning, good-intentioned parents, relatives, and advisors may have tried to protect us from our own immaturity and inexperience. They offered us wisdom and advice tempered with common sense that was intended for our own benefit. They tried to replace our naïve enthusiasm with traditional, practical values. In the process, they may have stifled some of the fantasies of our youthful minds.

One young student wanted to abandon his prep school studies that were preparing him for a medical or legal career in order to become an entertainer. He asked his school counselor for advice.

The counselor discouraged this student. He rightly observed that the youngster's grades were excellent. The teenager was an admirable candidate for any profession he wanted. The counselor felt it was unwise to abandon such a promising future for something as tenuous as show business.

The real death blow to the student's dreams, though, came with the advisor's closing sentence. He said, "Besides, what can you do?"

The advisor was right. This kid had no show business talent, but he did have desire. That drive could have prompted the lad to learn some skill or to perfect some talent. We'll never know.

My own dad's advice confounded me one time. I had saved enough money to buy myself a guitar. Dad said to me, "Why don't you learn to play a guitar before you spend all that money to buy one?" Dad was simply trying to keep me from spending foolishly, but it seemed logical to me that I should have a guitar to learn on if I were going to learn to play a guitar. However, I never purchased the instrument. (I probably wasted my savings on something equally as silly.)

Many of us have been talked out of some of our dreams by people whom we deem know better than we do.

2. Negative Peer Pressure:

John Ratzenberger, the actor who played Cliff on the TV show "Cheers," was recently a contestant on another TV show, "Dancing with the Stars." During an interview on that show, the host asked Ratzenberger if he had ever studied dance. He said (and I'm paraphrasing), "If one of the guys in my neighborhood said he was going to dancing lessons, those would probably be the last words he heard himself say."

Our companions can be cruel when we attempt something that doesn't fit in with their accepted practices. It's pack mentality. You do what everyone agrees is fitting for you to do or you suffer the consequences.

Some of our early desires may have been sacrificed so that we could fit in with the rest of the gang.

3. Fear of Outdistancing the Pack:

There's a negative reaction from friends and acquaintances when someone enjoys a success that they can't enjoy themselves. One schoolmate who was a couple of years behind me in elementary school was a good musician and became a protégé of a well-known bandleader. He once guested on "The Ed Sullivan Show." That was not only the talk of the school, but the entire neighborhood.

A few years later, he cut a record which got some play on the radio, but didn't rise too high on the charts. Again, though, we were all thrilled when we listened to "one of our own" on the radio.

Then he had a record that shot to the top. He became a big star. Were we thrilled? Not really. Most were more jealous of him than they were happy for him.

People resent it when you succeed and they don't.

I had a minor incident that illustrated this, too. I had worked at an industrial plant for thirteen years. When I got an offer to write for "The Jim Nabors Hour," someone rushed to the plant newspaper office to report that I was going to Hollywood. The editor of the paper was a good friend of mine. This "reporter" told the editor that I was going to write for Carol Burnett (which I wasn't at that time) and that my name was pronounced Per-ray (which it wasn't). He told her that my name was pronounced Per-ret, just like the little animal, the ferret. (My dad said Per-ray was the correct pronunciation but that we were never rich enough to say it that way.) The editor corrected this woman, but she insisted nevertheless that I was going to write for Carol Burnett and that my name was pronounced Per-ray.

A few days later, she returned and said, "You know that guy I told you was going to go to Hollywood to write for Carol Burnett? Well, he's gotten so snotty that he's changed his name to Per-ret."

Maybe we knew that we'd irritate our cronies by pursuing our dreams, so we didn't.

4. We're Too Young for That Vocation:

Advisors like to use this argument because we're helpless against it. We can't suddenly grow more mature. We are whatever age we are and we can't, at that moment, be any other age.

I wonder, though, if anyone told Tiger Woods when he was playing commendable golf at the age of six that he was too young to be a golfer.

Obviously there are professions that we can't enter until we reach a certain age, but that doesn't mean we can't begin our studies and our practice before then.

I was astounded once when a sports reporter interviewed Stan Smith when he was the number one tennis player in the world. He was asked about his preparation. He said (and again I'm paraphrasing), "It takes about five years to become a good tennis player and another ten years to become a great one."

That seemed like a long time to me. But it also seemed logical that if you wanted to become a world-class tennis player, you'd better start early—even when you're "too young."

Maybe some of us felt that our youth worked against us, so we abandoned a dream or two.

It seems, though, that I'm putting all the blame for abandoned ambitions on someone else. It was *their* fault. *They* did it to me. It sounds a little bit like Marlon Brando, the punch-drunk journeyman boxer in *On The Waterfront*. He complains to his powerful, controlling older brother, "I coulda been a contender."

It's also possible that we did it to ourselves. Let's take a look at some of these potential reasons.

5. Too Timid to Try:

There's a joke about a very devout priest who desperately needs money for his ministry. He prays that he will hit the lottery. That windfall will solve all his financial problems and allow him to continue to serve the needy. He doesn't win.

He doesn't get discouraged, though. He continues to pray. He still doesn't win.

Finally, he does get discouraged and angry. He's led a good life, he's done everything asked of him, and he's helped people who need his help. Why aren't his prayers answered?

Then one night God appears to him. Rather than being pleased with the visit, the cleric lashes out: "All I ask is to win the lottery. You can certainly do that for me, but no, You refuse to answer my prayers. I just don't understand it."

God says to him, "Sam, do me a favor. Buy a ticket."

We can't succeed if we don't try. Some of us were too timid to try. We wanted to be stars on Broadway, but we could never work up the courage to go to auditions. We wanted to become renowned novelists, but we never put anything on paper.

We may have allowed some of our fantasies to dissolve simply because we couldn't work up enough courage to try.

6. We Feared Failure:

And why didn't we try? Because we feared failure. Nothing is more embarrassing than failure. We knew that we couldn't fail if we didn't attempt. So we didn't.

Shakespeare said it well in Act I, Scene IV of his play *Measure for Measure*: "Doubts are traitors and make us lose the good we oft might win by fearing to attempt."

Ironically, some of us may have failed to reach our goals because we feared failing to reach our goals.

7. We Learned We Weren't Good Enough:

Hey, maybe you found out early on that you didn't have what it takes to do whatever it was you wanted to do. There's nothing wrong with that. If it's an honest evaluation, then it's a wise decision.

When I was in fifth grade I decided to try out for our elementary school basketball team. Normally only eighth graders played on the team, but my older brother was the coach of the squad so I figured I was a shoo-in.

At one point in the tryouts we all had to shoot free throws. I didn't have enough strength to reach the basket from the foul line. I tried several times but couldn't do it. Then someone suggested that I shoot the ball underhanded. Good idea, I thought.

I cradled the ball in both hands and then launched it upwards with all my might. The ball shot straight up in the air, hit one of the rafters in the gymnasium, ricocheted down, and clunked me in the head. My brother helped me up while all the other guys trying out for the team doubled up with laughter.

I decided on my own that I wasn't good enough to play on the school squad. That dream was wisely postponed.

8. The Price Was Too Great:

The renowned New York Jets quarterback, Joe Namath, once spoke at a banquet honoring Olympic gold-medalist Bruce Jenner.

At that roast Namath said (and again I'm reconstructing the comment), "Bruce Jenner and I have much in common. Bruce spent twelve years preparing for a career that lasted two days. I spent two days preparing for a career that lasted twelve years."

Namath was kidding about his own reputation for being a devil-may-care type of athlete, but he made a valid point—any goal we pursue has a price attached. One doesn't get to collect a first place medal without exhaustive preparation and training.

Any goal worth pursuing requires some sacrifice. Some of us decided early on that the price for our desires was more than we were willing to pay. I remember my mom cajoling me to eat my spinach. "You want to grow up to be a big, strong football player, don't you?" Yes, I did, but then I decided that maybe I'd pursue a vocation where spinach-eating was not a prerequisite.

Earlier I mentioned that my dad talked me out of buying a guitar, yet my parents did promote the study of music. I took violin lessons for awhile and also studied piano for a while. I say "for a while" because both of them required study and practice. I didn't want to sit in front of a piano or hold a fiddle under my chin for an hour a day, so learning music fell by the wayside.

You too may have to admit that you opted against some of your dreams because they simply required too much effort.

9. Other Dreams Occupied Our Time:

You probably had a laundry list of goals when you were younger. Most of us did. If we saw a football movie we wanted to grow up to be football stars. Watch a dance recital and we wanted to be ballerinas. I once saw a film about a saint and even decided to make that one of my ambitions (that one was abandoned quickly).

As I mentioned in the section above, I did want to learn music, but I couldn't afford to spend the required time practicing and studying because I had to be out on the field playing football or baseball, or in the gym playing basketball. These goals were more fun and perhaps more glamorous, so they took priority over music.

You also may have shunted some desires aside because others, at the time, seemed more...well...desirable.

10. Our Dreams Were Replaced by Better Ones:

We saw earlier that Life could be fickle, leading us along one path then suddenly changing its mind and guiding us along another. We can be fickle, too. Or maybe a better word would be "selective."

My grandsons played every sport that was offered. They signed up for Little League baseball, and they played on youth basketball teams. They played pretty well, too (if you can believe the unbiased opinion of a proud and doting grandfather).

They also played soccer. They signed up for the youngest leagues that were allowed. Although I knew very little about that sport, I attended every game that I could. Their grandmother and I stood on the sidelines when the game was very unsophisticated. Eight- and ten-year-old youngsters would chase after the ball wherever it went like a swarm of bees. As they grew older, they learned some of the strategies and played a game that looked a little more like soccer.

The point is that they discarded all other sports to concentrate on soccer. They made an informed and apparently wise decision to devote all their time and energy to soccer. It worked well for them. Both went on to play varsity soccer in college.

There's nothing wrong with having abandoned some ambitions in favor of others.

11. We Didn't Have the Time or the Money:

We're talking here about *really* not having the time or the money. Earlier I mentioned that I didn't have the time to study and practice my music lessons. As you well know, I had the time. I didn't want to spend it on a piano bench when I could be out playing second base. But neither time nor money is unlimited. Many of us had to spend both on things that were more important than chasing our fantasies.

These reasons—time and money—are so universal that we're going to devote separate chapters to them later in the book (Chapter 7 concerns time; Chapter 8 concerns money). For now, it's enough to recognize that one or both of these may have been the destroyer of some of our ambitions.

12. We Hit Our First Obstacle and Quit:

The Police Athletic League in our neighborhood offered boxing lessons at the local precinct. Several of my buddies and I rushed to the opening session. It was cool. They had a full boxing gym outfitted in the basement of the 41st precinct. There were heavy bags, light bags, and an actual boxing ring. We were thrilled. Boxing had now become another one of my childhood fantasies.

The police advisors tied boxing gloves on us and taught us the basics of the manly art of self-defense. We learned how to jab and how to parry the opponent's jab. It was all very rhythmical and clinical—almost like a dance routine. And rather easy.

Then they paired us off to step into the ring for a brief sparring session.

I faced off against one of my buddies. It was a great thrill to be in a real boxing ring. We jabbed and parried, jabbed and parried, jabbed and parried—precisely as we had been instructed.

Then my buddy hauled off and threw a wicked uppercut that splatted against my jaw and flung me to the canvas. The policeman immediately stopped the round and led me out of the ring. I wasn't knocked out, just surprised by the viciousness of the sucker punch.

However, when I looked in the mirror in the bathroom, all of my teeth were outlined in blood. That ended my dreams of being a boxer.

Every goal has obstacles. Sometimes we overcome them and proceed onward. Sometimes we quit right then and there.

13. We Simply Lost Interest:

As youngsters, our minds are constantly discovering new and amazing facts and learning about more and more interesting adventures. We're very impressionable and we tend to go with whatever is in front of us at the moment. What fascinates us this week may replace what fascinated us last week. This, too, may be replaced by something that is going to fascinate us next week.

I once knew a youngster who was fascinated with toy cars. He had an immense collection of miniature sports cars, fire engines, ambulances, pick-up trucks, and whatever else ran on four wheels.

He took this collection, housed in shoe boxes, wherever he went, and spent hours of uninterrupted joy playing with these toy vehicles.

Then one day (after a period of time) he stopped playing with them. They sat in the same shoe boxes on the top shelf of his closet. What happened? What changed? Nothing really. He simply lost interest in them.

The same thing can happen with our early desires—they just disappear. We move on to new goals and forget about previous ones.

14. We Decided on Our Own to Abandon Certain Dreams:

Sometimes we make a conscious decision to discard an ambition. Perhaps we mature a bit and realize that our fantasy is impractical or unattainable and we rightly and wisely decide to forgo it. Possibly somewhere along the way you, like me, realized that being a singing cowboy was not the profession you wanted to pursue.

Maybe you we're one of those fortunate few who had an abundance of options to select from. I think of Bo Jackson who was talented enough to excel in both professional baseball and football. Danny Ainge also played many years for the Boston Celtics of the NBA and for several years as an outfielder in major league baseball. Many of today's college athletes are good enough to be drafted by professional teams in various sports. They must make a choice. Which one will they concentrate on? You, too, may have had several career options. It's a nice dilemma to have, but you may have had to make a career choice. You selected and pursued your number-one priority, BUT numbers two, three, and four may still be alive somewhere in your soul.

Also, we're all entitled to change our minds. There's no guarantee that what you wanted when you were in fifth grade was what you wanted when you graduated eighth grade. What you dreamed of studying while you were in high school may not have been your major when you entered college. It could be too that what you got your college degree in was not the career you selected when you entered the work force.

Whatever vocational choice you made was purely that—a choice. There was no need to justify that choice. It didn't have to be the wisest selection. It was not even required that it be the best. What career you pursued was your decision. The ambitions that you discarded were your choices, too.

15. Infinite Number of Other Reasons:

The above is not an all-inclusive list. You may recognize a few of them as reasons why some of your ambitions melted away. But you may also have other reasons that are peculiarly your own. That's fine.

It's important to note that these are not condemnations of those people who dissuaded us from our goals. They're not a self-rebuke for anything you or I might have done to shelve an ambition. These reasons are not bellyaching or whining about any misfortune that befell our aspirations. The reasons above are neither good nor bad; they simply *are*.

Nor do they imply that everyone abandoned their desires. We noted earlier that many people have utilized their early dreams and have led full, exciting, rewarding lives. Tiger Woods, for example, was one, as was my classmate who went on to become a doctor.

They simply point out that there are real and valid reasons why some of our fantasies may have remained unfulfilled. However, as the title of this chapter suggests, *That Was Then.*

Now that we've reached the fifty-year milestone, we have a chance to revisit some of those "fallen by the wayside" aspirations. Now is our chance to realize a few of them, or if not to realize them, at least to attempt them. Give them the honest shot that they haven't had until now.

We've explored some of the reasons why our dreams may have dissolved in the first place. Now we have a chance to see if those reasons still obtain. We'll do this in the next chapter.

Chapter 3

This Is Now...

For whatever reasons—others discouraged us, we forgot about them, other activities crowded them out—some of our goals, wishes, and ambitions have fallen by the wayside. Now that we've reached the over-forty-nine mark, we get a second chance at them; we have an opportunity to round up those early goals and experiment once again with a few of them. It's like the proverbial second childhood.

Childhood is not a bad way to consider this activity. As youngsters we weren't hampered by reality or practicality. Back then, if we wanted something, we wanted it. And when we wanted it, we never considered that it wasn't obtainable.

As youngsters we were free from inhibitions and fears. We saw a dream and we chased it unabashedly and boldly. Then, of course, as John Lennon warned, Life intervened. For many years we've done whatever Life demanded while we may have been busy making other plans.

But we've played by Life's rules long enough. Now it's time for us to dictate to Life the rules by which we're now going to play the game. That childish bravado we once enjoyed can serve us well now.

Phyllis Diller is a legendary comedy performer. I'm sure you're all familiar with her delightfully humorous one-liners, punctuated by her infectious, raucous laugh. But you may not know that Phyllis is also an accomplished musician and a recognized artist.

Phyllis began painting and drawing seriously after she joined the over-forty-nine society. She took up this hobby as a time-filler for the long, lonely stretches on the road. Diller would carry her paints and pencils with her and spread them out on one of the beds in her suite. She joked, "It's sad when you're a single woman with double beds in your room and all you can fill one up with is art supplies."

My children presented one of Phyllis Diller's paintings to me as a Christmas present a few years ago. When Phyllis's daughter, Stephanie, took them on a tour of her studio, my kids asked her why Phyllis seemed to be so successful at so many various endeavors. Her daughter said, "No matter what Mom tries, it never enters her mind that she might not be successful at it."

That's the naïve, childish, unrealistic, impractical bravado that we should all try to recapture as we begin to unleash our creativity.

There was a commercial on television a few years back that said, "You only go around once in life, so grab for all the gusto you can." Well, it's true—we do only go around once in life, but that doesn't mean we're limited to only one grab for the gusto. No sir, we can keep grabbing and grabbing and grabbing again—as long as there are some things out there that we want.

Now, past forty-nine, we've already chosen certain career paths. We've amassed our "fortunes." Nevertheless, we've still got much time and energy to grab a little more gusto. We've still got the drive to pursue a few more dreams.

In the previous chapter we analyzed many possible reasons why our early wishes deserted us...or we deserted them. Those reasons were real and valid then, but as the chapter heading suggests, *This Is Now...*

Let's revisit those reasons to convince ourselves that now that we've passed our forty-ninth year, they no longer obtain. At least we'll see that they no longer have the same impact.

1. Adults Discouraged Us:

One adage tells us, "If you can't beat 'em, join 'em." That's exactly what we've done. Grown-ups once had a certain dominion over us because it was assumed they were wiser than we were. They had more hands-on experience than we had. They could predict the future better than we could. They knew what was good for us better than we did.

It's irrelevant now whether they were right or not. We have become them. There's no obligation to listen to *them* anymore. We can start listening to *ourselves*.

2. Negative Peer Pressure:

Once I joined a few fellow television writers for after-work cocktails. One of these gentlemen was a slave to the "in-crowd." His car had to be the most expensive; his clothes were designer brand names; his house had to be in the most exclusive neighborhoods. He would never buck the current, snobbish trends.

When the waitress took our drink orders, I asked for a manhattan. This fellow started laughing out loud and blurted out, "Who orders a manhattan nowadays?"

I said, "The people who want one."

It seemed to me that since I was the one who was going to drink the drink, I should be the one who should decide which drink I would drink—not the socialites of New York City or the Hollywood celebrities.

The same philosophy should apply to whatever it is we want to do. We've lived our lives for over forty-nine years now, largely without the concern of other people. If we want to do something now, we've earned the right to attempt it. It needn't be approved by "status police."

If you want a manhattan, order a manhattan.

If Phyllis Diller wanted to load that second double bed up with art supplies, she didn't have to check with her PR man to see if it would be *acceptable*. She just did it. If you want to pursue some creative activity, just do it. Don't fret about the opinions of others.

3. Fear of Outdistancing the Pack:

Bill Gates would probably admit to having once been a "geek." You remember from your schoolhood days what a geek was. We may have had a different slang word for it back then, but geeks were those kids who were always too busy studying or working on something that the "cool" kids thought was an horrendous waste of time. They were too busy studying music to come out and play in our sandlot pick-up football games. They were so occupied with perfecting their science project that they couldn't join the rest of the gang for hamburgers and shakes after school. They were the ones we ridiculed because we believed they were trying to do something better than the rest of us.

Well, Bill Gates may still be a geek. He happens to be, though, one of the richest geeks in the world. Had he gone along with the pack, chances are he'd still be one of them. That might make the pack happy, but it would have robbed Gates of considerable achievement and wealth.

We all have a chance now to do something that will satisfy us, not what people feel we should do to satisfy them.

4. We're Too Young for That Vocation:

Obviously, now that you've lived over five decades, you're not.

5. Too Timid to Try:

Unfortunately, we may not have outgrown our timidity. Even though we have over forty-nine years of productive living behind us, we might still be reluctant to attack a new creative adventure. Since overcoming this obstacle is not automatic, we must exercise a little bit of creativity to defeat it.

Try looking at the problem this way:

We've lived a lot and learned a lot. We succeeded in some things and fouled up others. Nevertheless, we're here. Therefore, the failures, as unpleasant as they may have been at the time, didn't destroy us. In fact, if we look at them realistically and honestly, we may have to admit that some of the setbacks may even have *benefited* us.

It's logical that we're still going to enjoy some successes and suffer a few defeats. When I began to study sculpting recently, my first project was a portrait. I handled the clay very timidly. When the instructor showed me some techniques, she would manhandle the clay. She'd shove aside huge amounts with her fingers and gouge out immense chunks with the sculpting tools.

I said to her, "I wish I had the courage that you have."

She said, "It's only clay."

That's a valuable lesson for those of use who are still nervous about attempting a creative project. Be bold. Be decisive. Be courageous. Why not? It's only an experiment.

6. We Feared Failure:

We're all attempting something relatively new to us and probably unfamiliar to us. There's a good chance we could fail. So what? Who cares?

I play golf with a group of retirees several times a week. We're all less-than-average golfers even on our good days. We exult in our occasional good shots and agonize over those shots that hook deep into the woods, splash into the water hazards, or clunk off the roof of an out-of-bounds (but not far enough out-of-bounds) home. We curse, slam clubs into the ground, and berate ourselves unmercilessly.

But you know what? When we gather for lunch after the morning's 18 holes, none of the other guys care:

"How'd you do today?"

"Oh, I had two holes in one."

"That's nice. Pass the ketchup."

Or:

"How'd you play today?"

"Aw, I played terribly. I lost eight golf balls and shot a 123."

"That's tough. Pass the ketchup."

Nobody really cares whether you played like Tiger Woods or Elijah Woods.

Keep in mind that failure in these creative endeavors is not catastrophic. Once I wanted to paint a very dramatic portrait of Bob Hope. I was using a photo taken from behind him while he was onstage and his portrait was highlighted by the spotlight out front.

I struggled with the technique, but finally finished the portrait and was rather pleased with my work. When I showed to it to my wife, she said, "It's nice, but why did you paint a picture of Jack Lemmon?"

I think I failed, but so what? Who cares? I painted over it.

7. We Learned We Weren't Good Enough:

This is a step beyond failing. If we fail at something—like painting a dramatic likeness of Bob Hope—we can always try again and perhaps succeed. If one of my golfing buddies does shoot 123 today, you know he's coming out the next day firmly believing he can break into the 90s. Admitting we're not good enough, though, is realizing that we're *never* going to succeed. That's powerful reality.

I dreamed of becoming a football player (I've dreamed of doing practically everything in my life). It's not going to happen. The National Football League offers very few tryouts to septuagenarians. It's discriminatory, but it's probably for the best.

We've lived fifty years of our lives now. We've succeeded in a few things and were mediocre or downright crummy at others. Somehow we got to this point in our existence. And you know what? We've all earned the right to not have to be good at everything we try.

I mentioned earlier that Dad dissuaded me from buying a guitar. Since then, though, I've studied a bit, but mostly I taught myself to play the instrument. I'm proud to say that today I'm one lousy guitar player. My wife kids me about my playing. She says that when I pick up my Gibson I can clear a room faster than a smoke alarm. Once I took my guitar on a long cruise and told my wife I was going to sit on deck and strum a bit. She said, "Be sure to wear your life jacket."

But I pick out a few tunes every day and I enjoy it.

Years ago if we spent time and money on a project, we expected it to pay some dividends. To fool around with something we couldn't be reasonably proficient at could very well cost us in other areas. As young adults fashioning our fortunes, we couldn't afford frivolous activities. Now we can.

If you take your grandkids out for a day of bowling, you don't expect them to rack up high scores. You probably won't, either. But I'll bet you and the youngsters will have loads of fun.

You don't have to be really good at something to reap rewards.

Once I attended a writers' conference. Charles Schulz, the cartoonist who created "Peanuts," was the featured speaker. In his cartoon panels, Snoopy had ambitions of becoming a famous writer. His novels would all begin with, "It was a dark and stormy night."

One of the attendees mentioned this to Schultz during a question and answer period and asked, "Will Snoopy ever sell any of his writing?"

Schultz immediately answered, "No." He explained that Snoopy was not good enough to become a marketable writer.

Later in that same session, someone recalled that exchange and said to Charles Schulz, "Many of us in this audience are just like Snoopy. We write a lot, but we're not good enough to sell anything. Should we continue?"

I felt sorry for the cartoonist because I thought he had painted himself into a corner, but he quickly offered this wise reply, "Yes, you should continue. The reward is in the doing."

Engaging in a creative activity, even after we concede that we're mediocre at best, can still be rewarding.

You don't have to be good at something to enjoy doing it.

Here's another possibility to consider—you just might surprise yourself and discover that you do have talent. Imagine the beauty the world would be missing if Grandma Moses had said to herself, "Oh, I'm too old to start painting and besides I'm probably not very good at it." She painted her first landscape when she was eighty-six years old.

It's possible that we can decide we're not good enough, but others will disagree with us.

8. The Price Was too Great:

Most achievement requires devotion, effort, and sacrifice. While we were busy carving out a livelihood for ourselves, we may not have been able to afford that type of sacrifice. Now, however, we've completed a considerable amount of that carving. We've put in the effort and endured the hardships. We've reached that point now where we are able to indulge ourselves.

Now is the chance for us to spend (and possibly waste) some time and money on those things we had to forgo earlier.

As a younger person your activities were expected to produce results—success, money, advancement. Today, though, those results are less important. The adventure, the fun, and the excitement are paramount.

When we mention "price," we're often talking about money or time. These are the most prominent and universal reasons for denying ourselves. They are substantial barriers. They were in the past and they may still be important considerations for many of us today. However, they are usually not unconquerable.

They are so dominant, though, that they deserve chapters all to themselves later in this book (See Chapters 7 and 8).

9. Other Dreams Occupied Our Time:

We've all had dreams fall by the wayside because *there were only 24 hours in a day*. Earning our daily bread was important, so some of our fantasies had to be abandoned. We selected only those goals that had the most potential. However, now is the time to resurrect a few of those ambitions. Maybe you couldn't go to art school and study medicine at the same time. Now, though, you can certainly buy a set of acrylics, a few brushes, and start pushing some paint around a canvas.

Consider your earlier dreams as not abandoned, but merely postponed—until now.

10. Our Dreams Were Replaced by Better Ones:

Yogi Berra, with his inimitable convoluted logic, once said, "When you come to a fork in the road, take it." And strangely enough, all of us have faced the "fork in the road" dilemma many times. We've had choices to make in life. Despite Berra's wisdom, though, it was impossible to travel along Path A and Path B at the same time.

If you selected Path A, you might wonder what fascination Path B might have offered.

Now that you've traveled a considerable distance along Path A, why not go back and explore a sampling of what Path B might have been like?

This is your chance to follow Yogi Berra's suggestion—take the fork in the road.

11. We Didn't Have the Time or the Money:

We've already touched on this somewhat under point 8 in this chapter. There are ways of budgeting both time and money, and we'll analyze them more fully, as I said, in Chapters 7 and 8.

12. We Hit the First Obstacle and Quit:

There are numerous stories of people who persevered through hardships and impossible circumstances to achieve a certain goal. The reports from Fred Astaire's Hollywood screen test supposedly said, "Can't act; can't sing; can dance a little." He wound up dancing a lot—also acting and singing quite a bit.

Sylvester Stallone wanted to sell a screenplay he'd written, *Rocky*, but only if he could star in it. The studios wanted the script, but not the actor. Stallone resisted all offers. He eventually outlasted the studios. He did star in the film and built a lucrative and long-lasting career largely on that initial performance.

Countless best-selling books were rejected many times before someone took a chance and published them.

However, there are also plenty of stories where people folded at the first sign of opposition. We all probably have a few of these in our own histories. It serves no purpose to revisit the "what might have been" of these tales. Nevertheless, there are likely a few where we wish we could.

It's too late to change history, but we still can revitalize some of the dreams we had back then, and give a few of them a second (or third and fourth) chance right now.

13. We Simply Lost Interest:

Sure, we've all changed our minds many times along the way. That's our prerogative. There's nothing wrong with substituting one goal for another. However, if a little bit of that spark of one of those dreams is still glowing—even faintly—why not try it again?

14. We Decided on Our Own to Abandon Certain Dreams:

We wisely discarded some of our early ambitions. Reasoning may have shown that they weren't really that worthwhile. We had other, more important, fish to fry.

But if you still feel like you'd like to fry a few of those other fish, now is the perfect time to try. You're old enough now to be independent and wise enough to make intelligent decisions. You've accomplished much to this point, but you've still got energy and enthusiasm enough to revitalize a few of those ambitions that you abandoned earlier.

15. Infinite number of Other Reasons:

There can be any number of reasons why our early dreams dissolved, disappeared, evaporated, or were simply forgotten. Only you know what your personal reasons may have been. I'll bet with a little thought and some common sense you can now find good reasons to pursue a few of them once again.

As a member of the "over-forty-nine crowd," you can infuse new life into some old ambitions. Why? Well, for several reasons:

You're more relaxed now. You've jumped over many of life's hurdles and have less at risk, so you can perform better now than you probably could have then. I notice when I play golf, some players will miss a relatively easy putt. Afterwards, they'll often drop the ball at the same spot on the green and putt again. Most of the time that second attempt will go into the cup.

There's no pressure on the second putt. The golfer relaxed and poked the ball with a solid stroke.

Whatever you're attempting is probably more fun the second time around. The first time you tried, it was probably stressful. It was important then that you did well. That sort of anxiety robs you of much of the enjoyment. Now you can relax and really enjoy the adventure.

You've matured, too. You're much more experienced. You know yourself better than you used to. You can persevere at whatever you're attempting because you don't get upset with less than magnificent results.

Earlier in your life, you did whatever you did for your future, for your family, for your fortune. Now you can do things for yourself. Enjoy them.

Chapter 4

More Reasons to Get Creative

We're not limited to merely resurrecting forsaken fantasies. Certainly, if there are projects you've always wanted to try, but never got around to, now's your chance. However, there are other substantial reasons for pursuing creative projects now that we've reached or passed the half-century mark.

1. To Relax:

I once played eighteen holes with a golf professional. Trying to sneak in a free lesson as we played, I casually asked him what he thought about while making his previous shot. I figured he'd offer some valuable tips about keeping his head still, turning his shoulders, swinging on an inside-to-outside plane, whatever. He said, "I thought about the same thing I always think about when I play golf—the money."

Golf was this man's livelihood. How much he earned depended on how well he scored. How well he scored hinged on how well he executed each shot. Consequently, the prize money influenced him on every swing.

We've all done the same thing. Perhaps not with golf, but with whatever we do for a living. There's pressure and stress connected with every profession. The guy who defuses bombs certainly has some nervous on-the-job moments. Brain surgeons deal with pressure each time they enter the operating room. But being the mother of a two-year-old who has to rush off to pick up her eleven-year-old twins to get one to his Little League game and the other to her soccer practice has a few stressful moments in her active day, too.

Often the stress takes different forms for different people. A musician friend of mine was having a pool built into his backyard. It was a scorchingly hot day, so he sat out back enjoying a tall glass of iced tea and reading a book. Meanwhile, the workmen were sweating away in the bottom of the unfinished pool.

During one of their breaks, one of the workmen asked why this gentleman had a phone by his side as he sat out in the sun. My friend replied that he was a musician and that he depended on phone calls for his various gigs.

The man wiped his sweaty brow and said, "Do you always have to be near a phone?"

The musician said, "Yeah. That's how I get work."

The laborer said, "Man, I wouldn't have your job for all the money in the world."

Different sorts of stress, but we all face some form or another in our workaday lives.

Years ago I worked as a draftsman and engineer at a large industrial plant. Just to get away from the 40-hour-a-week drudgery, I wrote comedy as a hobby. When writing gags, I had no pressing deadlines to meet. I had no bosses leaning over me telling me what to write and how to write it. I wrote because it was fun and relaxing. It got my mind off my work.

Then things happened. I sold a few jokes, began working for a few nightclub comics, and eventually was hired to write for national television. Very quickly, my relaxing hobby became a pressure-filled chore. One of my fellow TV writers once asked, "When did my career become a job?" I still enjoyed writing, but not all of the headaches that came with doing it for a living.

Now I needed a new, relaxing, creative hobby to take my mind off my writing.

We can all benefit from doing something that we enjoy for its own sake, and not necessarily for the results.

Many people take up golf as relaxation, yet if you've ever watched weekend golfers, you'd hardly believe the activity was relaxing. People curse after every other shot. Someone once said the game was called "golf" because all the other four-letter words were already taken. Hackers throw clubs, have fits of temper, and come home from the country club in a belligerent mood. This is relaxing?

Well, nobody ever said having fun was easy.

Nevertheless, even golf can be relaxing in its own demonic way. Yes, it can be frustrating. It can be stressful and irritating. However, you're getting irritated about something that *doesn't really matter*. It's a temporary kind of torture.

The relaxing part, as many golfers will tell you, is that while you're chasing that ball around the course—even if you're chasing it into forests and lakes—all you're thinking about is that devilish golf ball. You're not thinking about your 9 to 5, Monday to Friday woes.

Whichever creative activities you adopt may lead to setbacks and frustrations. You may try to paint a landscape and discover that the tree behind the barn looks more like a giant cucumber. You may try to write the Great American Novel, and after your first day's work, you wind up with nothing more than a title and a trash basket filled with rolled up, self-rejected, half-written pages.

That's OK, so long as you're having fun trying to do something you want to do.

2. To Try Something Different:

The late comedian Henny Youngman used to tell the following joke about his wife:

> *My wife said for vacation she wanted to go someplace she'd never been before. I said, "How about the kitchen?"*

There is excitement and adventure in visiting someplace different, a spot you've never been before. There's also a thrill in trying something new, an activity you've never attempted before.

A friend of mine told me he had tried free-falling from an airplane once.

I said, "Why?"

He said, "I just wanted to say I had done it."

He added, "I'll never jump out of a plane again—voluntarily—but now I can say I did it."

That's a good enough reason for you to explore an unfamiliar creative pursuit. It's an experiment. It should be fun to try. I think it was Will Rogers who said about the stock market, "If your stock goes up, sell it. If it doesn't go up, don't buy it in the first place."

So you may try something new just for the sake of trying something new. If it's fun, you just might continue doing it. If it's not fun, don't do it again.

The following tale has nothing to do with creativity, but it does illustrate that trying something different can sometimes be quite beneficial.

I'm not a big seafood fan—never have been. I refused to eat crab cakes. Friends would tout me on them, but I would just say, "No, I'll have a hamburger, thank you."

Then my wife and I went on a vacation with a group of friends. Everything was paid for in advance and the meals, with set menus, were included. At one dinner they served crab cakes as an appetizer. As much as I disliked seafood, I disliked even more paying for something and not getting it. I tentatively tasted the crab patties.

They were delicious!

Now my wife and I go to a local seafood restaurant every other week or so because that's about as long as I can go without indulging my craving for crab cakes.

Try something different; you might like it.

3. To Learn and to Grow:

Several reporters interviewed Bernard Baruch on his ninety-fifth birthday. He announced at the interview that one of his goals for the upcoming year was to learn to speak Greek fluently. One of the reporters asked, "Mr. Baruch, you're ninety-five years old. Why would you want to learn to speak Greek now?"

Baruch answered, "It's now or never."

* * *

One of the most memorable moments in my life was when I visited the World's Fair in New York and saw Michelangelo's magnificent sculpture of the Pietà. It was simply a chunk of rock, but it appeared so lifelike. There seemed to be a graceful movement in the marble itself. It was awe-inspiring.

Later I visited Italy and saw many great marble statues carved by Michaelangelo and other masters. To stand before the magnificently simple statue of David was worth the entire trip to Europe.

I enjoyed seeing all the great works of art in Rome, Florence, and Venice, but I was especially taken by the statues. How did artists work in a three-dimensional media like this? I knew in painting, if one feature didn't seem correct, you could paint over it. In drawing, you could erase mistakes. But in carving marble, if you accidentally forgot the nose, you couldn't go back and glue one on.

And I wondered how the bronze images were made.

So when I saw an ad in a local paper for an inexpensive course in sculpting, I signed up. It turned out not only to be educational, but also great fun. I learned some of the tricks that artists use to transform the clay into a portrait. Also, I learned the technique of converting the finished piece of clay into a bronze bust. It's a process—called "the lost wax" method—that has been used for centuries. It was in use for that long and I never knew about it—until I took a $90 class in sculpting with clay.

It's interesting that I went into this class having no talent for three-dimensional art and having no knowledge of the techniques of moving clay around or of creating a bronze art work. Neither one was a prerequisite.

All I really needed was a desire to learn.

Perhaps there are some questions that you'd like answered, too. Maybe there's some knowledge you wish you had but you don't currently possess. Maybe you'd like to know how bakers can maneuver the icing around to create such dramatically beautiful decorations on birthday and wedding cakes. Perhaps you'd like to know how to take two needles and a hank of wool and convert it into a cable-knit pullover sweater. Do you know how glass blowers convert molten liquid into beautiful vases or whimsical animal figures?

All of these things can be learned if you really want to learn them. As I've mentioned many times throughout this volume, now is the perfect time to grasp the fun of acquiring knowledge.

4. It's Good for What Ails You:

Creativity is a mental process. It's engaging in an activity that essentially begins in your mind. Some are purely intellectual activities. You can come up with a good premise for a novel while taking a shower. Perhaps you'll generate a useful new invention while enjoying your pre-dinner cocktail. Isaac Newton supposedly conceived his principles of motion while semi-snoozing under an apple tree. A falling apple clunked him on the head and gravity was born. It may not have actually happened that way, but it could have.

Other creative pursuits involve accompanying physical activity. If you come up with a creative idea for a fantastic pencil sketch, you will have to take a pencil in your fingers and move it around the paper. If you want to study ballroom dancing, at some point you're going to have to get on the floor and move your two left feet until one of them realizes it's actually your right foot.

Both purely mental and mental-physical exercises have therapeutic value. They both provide fringe benefits attached to whichever creative activity you engage in. We'll discus these benefits in Chapter 5.

However, you can also use the remedial benefits of creative activities in a more proactive way. You can use creative activities as a means of curing whatever ails you (or to prevent what you don't want to ail you in the future). This can be your reason for choosing a specific pursuit.

For instance, experts have advised that in order to keep your memory functioning and efficient, it's a good idea to engage in some mentally challenging hobbies. Doing crossword puzzles, sudoku, or trying to solve intricate word and logic puzzles is excellent therapy for the memory muscle. My aunt claimed that kneading dough provided some welcome relief from her troublesome arthritis. She made some delicious breads and baked goods. Pushing clay around in a sculpting class or learning to position your fingers on the neck of a guitar can help keep your fingers nimble and free from stiffness.

Which activity you should choose depends on whatever ails you (or whatever you want to keep from ailing you later). In fact, your ingenuity may help you to find a creative adventure that suits your circumstances. If you want to exercise the entire body, learning to tap dance or to cha-cha-cha may be more fun and more creative than working out at the gym.

If your mind needs a workout, as we mentioned, solving crossword puzzles can be helpful. To be even more creative, you might try writing crossword puzzles for others to solve.

If your doctor suggests a regular walking regimen, you can probably find a creative activity to make your strolls more enjoyable and more do-able. As a few *for instances*, you could make it a point to spot something during each walk that could be the basis for a short story or a poem. You might take along a camera and begin a creative photo collection. A friend of mine once determined to learn a new language. He wrote out a list of new vocabulary words that he would memorize during his daily hikes. He built up a sizable vocabulary in no time. His study made the walk more endurable and the stroll reduced the studying to less of a chore.

5. It's Something to Do:

For a few years, I lectured on cruise ships. My wife and I enjoyed visiting many fascinating ports and going on tours to exotic places. Mostly, though, we enjoyed the cruising. Each jaunt was like two or three weeks of floating relaxation.

The cruise lines pamper their passengers. Award-winning chefs prepare the customers' meals, meticulous maids tidy their rooms, and solicitous waiters deliver their cocktails. All the customers need do is show up, lie back, and enjoy.

Yet the schedule of each cruise day is packed full of activities. There are exercise classes on the forward deck, bridge tournaments in the lounge, putting contests on the aft deck, movies in the ship's theatre, bingo, art auctions, dance classes, Broadway shows, and lots of other time-fillers. Why? Because the cruise lines know that even though people are there ostensibly to relax, they also want something to do. The ship's staff knows that doing nothing can be fun, but folks often want something to do to help pass the time.

Reaching the half-century plateau is a bit like taking a cruise. We've certainly earned the right to occasionally sit back and do nothing. Still, we have the urge to do *something*.

That's as good a reason as any to start flexing your creative muscles. It's just something to do.

6. Just Because You Want to:

The lovable comedian, George Burns, used to kid about his longevity. He'd say, "When I get up in the morning, the first thing I do is read the obituary page. If my name's not in there, I shave."

An interviewer, though, once asked Burns how he managed to live such a long life and remain so vibrant and active despite his advancing age. George replied, "I'm happy to begin each new day because I look forward to doing not only what I want to do, but what I love doing."

George Burns lived to be over one hundred years old doing what he wanted to do. That's probably the best reason for doing something creative. In fact, it's probably the best reason for doing anything at all—*because you want to.*

Chapter 5

Why Bother?

Years ago, in my hometown of Philadelphia, the Philadelphia Athletics (known to all their fans as "the A's") played baseball in the American League. The National League team was the Phillies. All Philadelphia residents had to root for one team or the other, but never both. Our family were devoted Phillies fans. At the end of each day of baseball season, my dad would grab the sports page, pull out his loose-leaf books, sit at the kitchen table, and carefully record the statistics of all of the Phillies players. He wrote all the details into his books by hand and did all the computations in his head. Remember, this was in the pre-computer age.

I would ask myself then, "Why bother?"

Dad knew what each player was batting, how many singles, doubles, and triples he had. He could tell you the number of errors each fielder had made and how many assists he had to date.

Dad never published any of his stats. In fact, he rarely mentioned them even when we discussed what the Phillies did that day or how they were doing in the current pennant race.

He just kept his statistics.

Why did he bother to do it? *Because he wanted to do it*. He enjoyed it. It gave him something to do each evening. In a sense, it made him part of his favorite team.

Were these good reasons? They didn't have to be. Dad wanted to keep his hand-generated stats; so he did. That was reason enough.

You may be wondering why you should bother with a creative activity. Well, whatever reason you may have doesn't have to be justified. If you want to do it, do it. However, there are many valid benefits associated with whatever activity you choose. Let's look at a few of them.

1. They Have Therapeutic Benefits:

Once again, we turn to the gentle wisdom of George Burns, who used to boast about the shape he was in despite his age. The beloved comedian used to joke in his act, "I can do anything at eighty that I could do at eighteen. Which gives you an idea of what terrible shape I was in when I was eighteen."

Bob Hope said, "You're only as young as you feel. And I don't feel anything until about noon. By then it's time for my nap."

Phyllis Diller cheated the aging process many times by having cosmetic surgery. Someone asked her once how old she was. She replied, "Which part of me?"

Now that we've hit the round number of fifty, we have to think about maintaining the supple body and the nimble mind we've enjoyed to date. In the previous chapter we mentioned that one of the reasons for seeking out some creative activity was because it is good for what ails you. In that discussion we actively sought out an activity that would benefit what ailed us.

Even without that incentive, every creative activity pays therapeutic dividends, whether we seek them out or not. They're simply a bonus that comes with the activity.

Creativity gets your mind working and keeps it exercising. This has to have long-lasting beneficial results. Anything that you do repeatedly keeps you fresh and sharp.

Physical activities provide corresponding physical results. You may take up tap dancing just because you like it. That's fine, but it's still going to provide a pretty good cardiovascular workout. Hiking around a flea market may be a great way to discover some antiques or find some interesting items for your unique collections. It's also providing some very pleasant and healthful walking at the same time.

There's a saying I'm sure you've heard—"Anything I like is illegal, immoral, or fattening." Creative activities should be none of the above. They should be entertaining, and, like it or not, good for you.

2. They Keep Us Productive:

There comes a time when we're no longer the important cog in the wheel that we used to be. I recall how dramatically "Dad's Day" at my daughter's college drove this point home to me. The kids invited us fathers to campus, partied with us on Friday night, took us to the big football game on Saturday afternoon, and treated us to dinner after the game. It was great fun, but it was somewhat demoralizing to realize that this youngster was now pretty much on her own. I was once the authority figure, the guiding force in her life. Now I was just one of the "cute" dads.

It happens in our work life, too. It happens almost everywhere. Look at athletes. They have a relatively short productive life span. Henry Aaron was a great home run hitter. Michael Jordan was an unbelievable force in basketball. Martina Navratilova was almost unbeatable in tennis. Today, none of them can compete with the younger, quicker, more agile sports stars. They can no longer produce championship results.

It can be frustrating. And it can't be recaptured. But it can be replicated in other areas. That's how a new creative activity can lift your spirits.

When you're painting a picture, you're central. You're totally in charge. You're the one who will get the task accomplished. That's a magnificent feeling.

If you're building a model of a ship, you're in command. You're the captain of this vessel. You're in charge of everything—from gluing the pieces together right down to the finish coat of paint and applying the last decal.

It's nice to be a productive force. As Mel Brooks says in one of his films, "It's good to be king."

3. They Fulfill Our Need for a Challenge:

During Rita Rudner's Las Vegas act, she once commented on a woman who swam completely around Manhattan Island. Rita said,

"When they asked her why she did it, she said, 'Because it's never been done.' If she wanted to do something that's never been done before, she could have vacuumed my apartment."

Most of us welcome a challenge. We play golf to see if we can score well against par. We gamble not to get rich, but to see if we can beat the odds. We bungee jump...well, I don't know why anybody bungee jumps.

Facing a challenge invigorates us. It gives us a reason to suit up for the game. It keeps us vital and involved.

Engaging in a creative activity can provide the same thrill.

4. They Take Our Mind off Other Concerns:

One hospital held a banquet each year for those people who were going through the heart rehabilitation routine. At this banquet they would have trophies for those hardy (no pun intended) souls who could pass the 12-minute mark on the treadmill stress test, those who were the most congenial in the rehab sessions, and other awards.

The speaker at this dinner one year was a humorist who kidded the whole practice. He said, "The doctor who performed my surgery is at this banquet tonight. I happened to glance over at him during the meal and his wife was cutting his meat for him."

He also told a story about having to pedal on the exercise bike for a half-hour. The nurses in the rehab room were driving forces. They would push the patients to keep improving. He told of one time when he was whining:

"I was riding this exercise bike and I kept complaining. The nurse told me to keep going, keep pedaling. I whined and griped, and I pleaded for relief. The nurse would hear none of it. He made me keep going, and going, and going. Finally the half-hour was up and we found out what the problem was. The seat had fallen off my bicycle."

After the appreciative laughter died down, he added, "It took my mind off my heart problems, I'll tell you that."

It was a funny story, especially to an audience of people who were struggling through these rehab routines three times a week. The anecdote also contained a message that has meaning for us— activity can distract you from other thoughts.

That's one of the blessings of any creative activity that you enjoy—it keeps you totally absorbed in whatever you're doing. When you're concentrating hard on your pastime, you don't think about other problems that may otherwise concern you.

Of course, any activity you pursue has its own problems and concerns built into it. If you're playing golf, you might have to figure out how to hit under a tree, over a water hazard, and try to miss a sand trap all at the same time. If you're painting a portrait of George Washington and it's beginning to look more like Abraham Lincoln, that's a problem. However, most of these concerns will be trivial compared to other day-to-day concerns. And even if they're not, it's often beneficial to take your mind off one set of complications by focusing on another. Just the change of pace can be a welcome relief.

5. They Provide Social Benefits:

At a roast one humorist kidded the guest of honor. He said, "This man doesn't have an enemy in the world. However, a lot of his friends don't like him." Friends, whether they like us or not, are an important asset to all of us. And many times we can't depend on our "old friends." Time and circumstances have a way of separating us from our closest cronies.

In the TV writing profession, there was hardly any stability. Shows got cancelled, staffs were changed, people moved onto other assignments. When we separated, we'd always say, "Let's get together for lunch," and we'd always mean it. Yet somehow the lunches never happened. Our office mates and close buddies would soon become memories.

A creative activity introduces you to many new friends. Even if the activity is a solitary one, you'll usually find ways of meeting other people who share your interest. You'll meet them at local meetings, or at seminars and conventions.

Sometimes the dividends pay additional dividends. When my wife and I moved to a new location, I decided to try golf, a game I had never really been involved in. I began playing with a group of about twenty-five to thirty golfers. Several of us would meet each morning at a given time, we'd split up into teams, we'd play eighteen holes of very casual competitive golf, and then we'd enjoy lunch together. They became the social nucleus of our new neighborhood.

We'd also get together periodically for dinner or a party. My wife met the wives of my golfing friends and now she plays bridge with some of the wives on certain days. She joins another group on other days for dominoes.

I not only found a new group of cronies through my new activity, but my wife formed many close friendships, too.

6. They Can Offer Practical Benefits:

If you can knit or sew, you can create beautiful articles of clothing. If you can crochet, you can have gorgeous tablecloths or doilies around the house. If you're skilled with woodworking, you can make your own pieces of furniture. In fact, with some inventiveness you can often find useful applications for virtually any creative endeavor you engage in. For example, if you take up cake decorating, you can provide personal cakes for your family and friends on their birthdays. Rather than just a cake that says "Happy Birthday, Charlie," you can create a unique design that applies specifically to good old Charlie. You might even incorporate an inside joke into your design.

One gentleman, a frustrated joke writer, would always produce a comedy book for special occasions. For a friend's anniversary or birthday or promotion or whatever, he would collect some silly pictures from magazines or newspapers—sometimes he'd even gather family photographs—and then assemble them into a loose-leaf book with witty captions for each photo. They always delighted guests at the function and had a very special, personal meaning for the guest of honor.

I mentioned my golfing group in the above section. Each year this group has a Christmas party at the club where we play. Generally, I do a short monologue "roasting" them about their golf. I kidded one of our more erratic golfers who always walks the course, rather than renting a cart. I said of him, "He doesn't really need a golf cart. Where he hits the ball, it's easier to take public transportation."

This year, though, I'm combining one of my newer creative activities with my comedy writing. I'm going to present the golfers with "jokes-to-go." I've taken a few photographs of each of the guys and will convert them to pencil sketches—my new hobby. Each drawing will have a humorous caption written across the bottom. It should be a surprise and it should be fun.

No matter what creative activity you choose, you can find some sort of practical application for it.

7. They Can Provide Financial Benefits:

Yes, it's OK if your new pursuit adds to your income. In fact, for some it's the reason why they choose it. A friend of mine toyed with an acting career when he appeared in community theatre productions as a youngster to help overcome a stuttering problem. However, it never developed into anything worthwhile. In college, when he auditioned for several roles, the best he could land was one line in *King Lear*. Discouraged, he abandoned his theatrical ambitions.

Later, though, at about the age of fifty, he needed money for various family medical expenses, so he auditioned for several professional acting roles at a local dinner theatre. He landed the second lead as Captain Andy in *Show Boat*. This led to a long and profitable *secondary* career in professional and semi-professional productions in the Philadelphia area.

He resurrected an earlier ambition because he needed the extra cash. It paid off in money and the enjoyment of being the actor he hoped he would one day be.

Mae Laborde became an actor even later in life. It has paid off handsomely for her also. You may have seen her on television. She's appeared on "MADtv," "Real Time with Bill Maher," and several national commercials. Her windfall happened almost by accident.

A Los Angeles columnist did a human interest story about her in which he sought out some lighthearted driving tips. She was still driving around Los Angeles at the age of ninety-four. A Hollywood agent saw the piece, had lunch with Mae Laborde, and ended the meal by signing her as a client.

So, whether you're trying for the cash or it just happens to come your way, it can be a nice fringe benefit that accompanies your creative activities.

8. They Can Open up New Vistas:

Remember earlier we quoted John Lennon: "Life is what happens to you while you're busy making other plans." Well, those things that Life presents to you, almost without your consent or approval, are not always negatives. They can be genuine blessings. The creative pursuits you begin now can lead you along paths that you might never have considered or even dreamed possible.

In fact, this book you're reading now is an example. I've mentioned before that I was interested in sculpting, so I signed up for a class in a nearby art center. The sculpture piece I worked on turned out to be not all that bad (thanks largely to my instructor's input and guidance), so I had it made into a bronze bust. I've also mentioned that I recently began studying music so I could play guitar with a bit more knowledge and confidence.

In a conversation with my publisher I mentioned these activities (I somehow manage to mention them to everybody in every conversation). He said it was interesting that he was considering doing a book called *Unleashing Your Creativity After 50*. I said, "That sounds fascinating. I might enjoy writing a book like that."

Within a month, we signed the contract.

Once you start an activity, there's no predicting where it will lead you. This time I'll re-quote Yogi Berra—"When you come to a fork in the road, take it." Oftentimes, Life takes you past that fork in the road without your even being aware of it.

Some of the benefits you may reap from unleashing your creativity are unknown to you. They're out there in the future. They're part of the Life that happens to you while you're busy making other plans.

They can lead to interesting adventures, though. Enjoy them.

9. They're Fun:

This chapter started out with me wondering why my dad bothered to keep all those ball player statistics night after night. Why bother? I asked.

Dad did it because it was fun. That's a pretty intelligent, substantial, legitimate, irrefutable reason for doing anything. So pick out a creative activity that you'll have fun pursuing, and start doing it.

Chapter 6

Still Not Convinced?

This is a wonderful time to revitalize some of your childhood dreams and fancies and give yourself a second chance at them. All the excuses you once had have likely been dispelled and there are a host of benefits for you if you'll just try. Nevertheless, some people still find reasons why they shouldn't get too aggressive.

"I don't think I'm good enough to do that." You know what? You may not be. But you know what else? Nobody cares. You know something else? You just might be good at it, but don't know it yet.

Grandma Moses was a self-taught artist who didn't start painting until she was in her eighties. She didn't think she was that good, either. She sold one of her paintings in 1942 for $110. That same painting was recently assigned an insurance value of $60,000.

Besides, who's to say what is "good enough." I have some paintings that I consider priceless. They're not valuable; they're priceless. Some were done by my children, others by my grandchildren. They may not wow the art critics or demand record-breaking sale prices at auctions, but they hang proudly in my home.

People may value your work not because of its intrinsic value, but simply because you did it. To them, that's "good enough."

Remember, too, the story of Charles Schulz telling an audience of writers that Snoopy was not good enough to be a professional writer. Some in the audience felt that they weren't good enough, either. Schulz told them it was no problem—"The reward is in the doing."

Suppose, though, you discover that you truly are not good enough to do what you're attempting to do. That's OK, too. There is a benefit in learning that. It is said, "It's better to have loved and lost than never to have loved at all." This book isn't about your love life, but we can paraphrase that saying—"It's better to have tried and failed than never to have tried at all."

If you try and don't succeed you know it's not what you were meant to do. Now you can dismiss that endeavor. What you want to avoid is looking back and saying to yourself, "Boy, I wish I had tried that."

"I'll look silly if I try something new at my age." Ruth Mayerson Gilbert, who died in 2007 at the age of ninety-seven, looked silly when she tried something new. She bought her first camera when she was sixty-two and didn't know how to use it. She loaded the first three roles of film into it incorrectly and all the photographs she took came out totally black. That's about as amateurish as you can get.

Within ten years of that *silly* beginning, her photography was being acclaimed by experts. There's no shame in looking ridiculous while you're learning.

Phyllis Diller, who has tried several creative activities in her lifetime, once said that there is no such thing as a good beginning comic. She said, "They're all terrible." Phyllis included her own formative years in this condemnation.

You almost have to look silly when you're learning a new skill. It takes a while to find your voice, to learn the nuances of the craft.

So looking silly is not an excuse. It's a statement of fact—for a while anyway.

Another thought on this same excuse. It's very easy to avoid looking silly—don't tell anybody you're doing it. If you want to try needlework art, try it. If it turns out beautiful, show it off proudly. If it turns out awful, rip it out or toss it out. Start a new one, or take up a different creative activity.

Also, what do you care what people think? Folks may indeed say, "You're wasting your time with that dumb pastime of yours." The response to that is, "I'll make you a deal. You do what you want with your time and money and I'll do what I want with my time and money. Deal?"

We sometimes hamper ourselves with false assumptions. You have no guarantee that others will look on your creative efforts as "silly." They may applaud you and praise you for being wise and courageous.

And finally, you've lived and worked for over half a century. You've earned the right to be "silly." Enjoy it.

"I'm too old to be trying anything new." Bob Hope used to talk about George Burns's dedication to his profession even when he was in his nineties. Hope used to say, "George Burns is ninety-five years old. He just signed a five-year contract with Caesar's Palace. George said they wanted him to sign a ten-year contract, but he refused. He said that would be silly. 'How do I know they'll be around in ten years?'"

That's a comedic story, but it does have a serious message—don't ever consider yourself *too old* for anything. One woman was considering going back to college to earn her bachelor's degree even though she was nearing fifty. When someone asked her about it, she confessed that she abandoned the idea.

"Why?" this person asked.

She said, "It's a dumb idea. If it takes me four years, I'll be fifty-two when I graduate."

The friend asked, "And how old will you be in four years if you don't graduate?"

* * *

"But wait a minute," you may argue. "Surely the ship has sailed on some of my ambitions." The cavalier—maybe pollyanna-ish—response to that is "It's never too late." That wouldn't really be an honest or practical statement, though. Yes, there does come a time when certain ambitions have to be considered unattainable. Now that I'm in my seventies I might still from time to time dream of starring for the Philadelphia Eagles as a speedy, flashy running back. It's not going to happen. The NFL doesn't hand out many bonuses or contracts to seventy-year-old rookies.

That still doesn't mean that I can't realistically pursue some part of that dream if I wanted to. It might be a thrill for me to become the home-field announcer for the local high school football team. Maybe I could even be a part-time coach helping out with the high school varsity or JV team. I certainly could buy into a fantasy football team of my own and maybe coach my guys to a championship season—even if it is only virtual reality.

Some dreams may indeed slip out of our grasp, but with some creativity, we should be able to grab some facet of that dream and still keep busy and have fun with it.

* * *

However, there are still a couple of excuses that seem to be fairly powerful deterrents. Let's discuss them in the next two chapters.

Chapter 7

Not Enough Time?

Remember Bob Hope's retort when someone asked him what he would change if he had his life to live over again? He said, "If I had my life to live over again I don't think I'd have the time." As with most wit, it had an element of truth in it. Think about your own life. Look at all you've accomplished in your fifty-plus years. How did you ever find the time to get all of that done? It's almost unbelievable to imagine the amount of achievement we can pack into our allotted 24 hours a day.

But it's that allotment that makes budgeting our time seem so impossible. We're dealing with a finite amount. It's the ultimate "fixed income." Each of us gets only 24 hours a day. We can't buy more. We can't bargain for more. We can't steal more. We get our 24-hour-a-day stipend and we have to make do with that.

Time also is not as flexible as money. It doesn't pay interest or dividends. We can't coax time to generate more time as we can with money. If you pay $2 for an item and sell it for $3, you've made a buck. You can't do that with time.

We can't accumulate time. We can't deposit it in a bank for safekeeping or lock it up in a safe deposit box for whenever we feel we need it. Time comes and it goes. Once gone, it's not retrievable and it is rendered useless. Wise men have always recommended "saving something for a rainy day." With time, when a rainy day hits, it's the same as any other day—24 hours long.

One advantage of time is that we get a renewable, steady, dependable input. As soon as one hour goes by, we get another one. There's no poverty with time. You'll never run out of it for as long as you live. Regardless of what we do with our time, it's constantly being replenished.

So, again, we get 24 hours a day, every day. There are no restrictions on the time we're given. We can use it any way we wish. However, what we don't use, we lose—forever.

Time is very fair, too. All of us—rich or poor, male or female, smart or dumb, ambitious or lazy—get the same *per diem*. There are no taxes withdrawn, no fees attached, no house percentage we have to pay. One hundred percent of our time income is there for us with no strings attached, no small print in the contract.

It's ironic that even though each of us knows exactly how much time we have available to us and how dependable and steady our allotment is, we still complain, "I just don't have enough time."

Let's look at ways that we can manipulate time, use it more efficiently, or *trick* ourselves into believing that we have more than we really have. Let's investigate how we can use the time we do have to enjoy some of the creative projects we'd like to explore.

1. Steal Time from One Project to Give to Another:

This is the old "rob Peter to pay Paul" ploy. My dad used to illustrate this idea with a story about an Indian who was too tall for his blanket. He would go to sleep at night, but when he pulled the covering up to his chin, his feet were exposed. It was hard for him to sleep with freezing feet, until one day his squaw solved the dilemma. As my dad tells it, she cut four inches off the top of the blanket and sewed them onto the bottom of the blanket—where it was needed. From then on his feet were nice and warm and he slept well.

There's a bit of logical illogic to that tale. My dad told it—like most of his other fables—for comedy effect, but it does have a moral to it. Even if you honestly don't have enough time for a new creative activity, you probably have some *unused* time in various other projects. It's possible that you can gather some or all of that time, accumulate it, and generate more time for creative pursuit.

Let's create a hypothetical to illustrate this point. Suppose you want to do some pencil drawing but you just can't find the time. Your day is too busy, and in the evening, you enjoy watching television. That's a relaxation you've certainly earned and are entitled to. Let's suppose, further, that you have one favorite show that airs from 7 to 8 o'clock. The show that is on from 8 to 9 is OK, but not one that you can't miss. Your real *gotta watch it* show is broadcast from nine to ten. Perfect. From 8 o'clock to 9 you can sit in front of the TV, maybe hit the mute button, and do some sketching while your OK show is on TV. You're not really missing anything, and you're sneaking in a little of the work you want to get done at the same time.

Here's one way that I can steal lots of time from one project and give it to another. Let's say I'm building a model airplane, but there's a great boxing match on TV that I would like to see. Television is great for expanding big events so that they become even bigger. I remember one comedian who talked about watching the Super Bowl one year. Before the game the network had extensive pre-game activities featuring flag waving, marching bands with patriotic themes, dancers prancing all over the field waving red, white, and blue banners, and rock stars singing all sorts of songs praising America. This comic said, "I don't know about you, but after two and a half hours of this, I was getting sick of 'Freedom.'"

The Olympics feature as many "Up Close and Personal" segments as they do the actual sporting events. Boxing, especially the more important matches, has interviews and documentaries, and all sorts of filler material before they get around to the actual fight.

So, I went to my den, worked on my model aircraft, and taped the fight on my VCR. Later that evening, when I had completed whatever work I wanted to do on my model building, I watched the fight. I skipped over all the *non-fight* stuff, and even hit the fast forward button between rounds.

I can condense two to three hours of broadcast time into maybe a half-hour of watching actual boxing.

With a little creativity, you can steal from one project to make time for another. You can keep your feet nice and toasty by cutting a bit off the top of the blanket and sewing it onto the bottom.

2. Combine Some Activities:

Many of the things we do during the day don't require our full attention. There are a few klutzes in the world who can't walk and chew gum at the same time, but most of us can. If we can combine efforts, we can do two things in half the amount of time it takes to do them separately.

A friend of mine once said, "There's a good basketball game on tonight. That's good. I can get my exercise in."

I said, "What?"

He said, "I never find time during the day to walk on the treadmill. But if there's a game on, I turn on the TV, switch on the treadmill, and walk leisurely while I watch the game."

Earlier I mentioned the man who learned new vocabulary words for the language he was studying while he went for his daily stroll. He didn't need time to exercise and time to study; he simply needed exercise/study time.

Once I promised my four youngsters that I would take them to see a new movie that was playing in only one theater in town—an hour's drive from our house. Just a short time before we were about to leave, I got a call from a client to write some comedy material. It had to be delivered almost immediately.

My kids were disappointed and a bit angry with me that I would have to renege on my promise. However, I told each of them to grab a small notebook and a pencil or pen. We were going to go to see that movie.

When we got buckled into the car for the hour drive to the theater, I told the oldest one to write down the first thing I said. The next oldest was to write the next item I dictated. And so on down the line. When we got to the youngest, we'd simply start the pattern over again.

As we drove, I dictated jokes. The kids wrote them down. During the hour drive, I had generated enough material to satisfy my client. When we got to the theater, the youngsters bought some popcorn and drinks and went in to watch the film. I gathered their notes, assembled them into some sort of logical order, and called the client's office from the pay phone in the lobby. Obviously, this was before cell phones became the rage.

I had combined the activities of driving to the theater with writing comedy. It worked well. It not only *saved* me some time, but it also saved my reputation as a good daddy.

3. Plan Your Creative Activity:

Organizing your project and mapping out a schedule can be invaluable in an efficient and effective use of whatever time you do have available.

As a television producer working with freelance writers, I would always ask for an outline before they began writing the script. It kept them on target and as they progressed they knew exactly how much more work they had to complete in order to meet their deadline. It kept the writing more consistent. Writers wouldn't hand in a first scene of twenty-five pages followed by a second scene of four pages.

The following are a few of the benefits good planning can contribute to whatever activity you choose:

a. With a step-by-step plan you can more readily see what must be done, in what order, and with a good idea of how much time will be involved. You can pretty much tell at a glance what you want to do on this project right now and how much time you're going to have to set aside to complete that segment of the project. Also, once you know how much time you'll need to complete a certain segment of your activity, you can *make time* for that in your daily schedule.

b. The plan will break your project into *chunks*. This makes it easier for you to attack your project whenever you find yourself with a bit of time to use. You won't have to waste part of that time trying to figure out how to best use it. Sometimes when a person can't figure out what to do on a certain project, they wind up doing nothing at all. If you have a plan, you can just glance at it, and it will tell you what you have left to complete and suggest which segment you should attack next. (You'll also see that a plan of some sort will help you when you come to Item 6 in this chapter.)

c. A plan helps you avoid wasted time and duplicated work. Earlier I mentioned that as a producer I required an outline before giving a go-ahead to writers for a script. Without some sort of road map, writers would often get carried away with their own creativity and genius. They could get "on a roll," as comedy writers say. They could write a brilliantly funny and compelling first scene that went on for many more pages than the time constraints of television would allow. Sure, when they were inspired, they wrote well and they wrote quickly. However, the scene was much too long. It was more trouble and time to go back and edit the scene down to size, and that involved doing one task two, or maybe even three times. That can't be time efficient.

d. A step-by-step plan can help you make good use of "down" time in a project. By down time, I mean those periods where for some reason or another you can't simply keep going. For instance, in furniture making, you may have to glue pieces together and clamp them into place until the glue dries. You can't do anything until the glue sets and you can remove the clamps. That's down time. Almost every activity has some down time (and we'll discuss this more in Item 6 of this chapter). However, there are often other facets of the project that you can work on while the glue is drying—even if it's only more planning. By having a well-organized schedule, you can see what other facets could be attended to during down time.

This planning doesn't have to be a major clerical undertaking. It might be a detailed formula written out on paper or in your computer. It might, though, simply be an informal plan that you have tucked away in the back of your mind.

Let me give some examples:

> When I begin to write a book, I plan the entire process chapter by chapter. I write out a brief description of what each chapter will cover. Since I know how many chapters I'll have in the finished book and how long the publisher wants the book to be, I know approximately how many words should be in an average chapter. Next I plan how many chapters I have to complete each week in order to meet my contractual deadline. Using this plan I can keep track of my progress and not wind up one week from the deadline with 75 percent of the book still not completed. With this detailed plan I can isolate segments of the writing. For instance, I might spend one afternoon thinking through and making notes on Chapter One. The following day I might take those notes and convert them to text. Next I might outline Chapter Two, or perhaps Chapter Ten, and then type those notes into the manuscript.

This is a quite detailed, organized plan and it serves me well in completing a book that is logical, comprehensive, and gets finished on time.

An example of a less formalized, yet effective plan, would be in completing a painting. The artist knows that she must first sketch out the scene, either on canvas or in her head. Then she arranges the facets of the painting into a logical sequence. When the sky is painted in, she can then work on the mountains. After that, perhaps she could add the green grass and the bushes. Then she might plan the trees and so on.

This is certainly not as rigid as the book schedule, but it is an actual plan and can be a great aid to the artist in completing the painting.

Your plan can be as detailed or as relaxed as your creative activity demands. Also, much of the planning depends on your personality and style. Nevertheless, some sort of road map should help you to use your time more wisely and thus create more of that time that we all claim we don't have enough of.

4. Set an Inflexible Time for Your Creative Activity:

The best way to get anything done is to do it. When someone asked Phyllis Diller what advice she would have for someone who wanted to begin a creative activity, she said, "Start it!" Then she added, "And finish it, too."

One sure way to start a project, continue a project, and then complete a project is to set aside a regular time to work on that project…and then stick to it. Most youngsters at one time or another have taken music lessons. Not too many of them, though, stick with it long enough to become competent. Which ones do? Those who were either willing to, or were forced to practice regularly. The ones who sat at the piano tapping out scales for a half-hour a day eventually learned to play the piano. That discipline helps.

Also, the regimen aids in finishing the task. Anne Lamott wrote a book entitled *Bird by Bird: Instructions on Writing and Life*. She explains the unique title by telling a story about her brother who had to complete a report for school on hundreds of birds. He kept postponing the assignment. When the report was due, he was overwhelmed with the seemingly impossible task of writing about the various species of birds in one sitting. He asked his dad how he could do it. The father said, "Bird by bird."

We're all guilty of procrastinating. We put off what should be done today until tomorrow. Then finally we hit that last tomorrow when all of yesterday's assignments are due today.

By scheduling a regular time to perform whatever activity you've selected, you start accumulating results. You keep chipping away at the assignment so that you're never faced with the impossible.

he treats over
people who
50 like them
don't work
or are
self-emp

5. Schedule Your Work when You're most Productive:

Most things are cyclical, including us. The sun rises and gives off light during the day, then, as one comedian once said, "At night, the sun gives off dark." Tides rise and fall. The seasons go from spring to summer to fall and to winter. Each of us, too, follows a pattern of energy and weariness. The trick to making the most of your time is to capitalize on those periods of vigor.

We do this by using the natural patterns. We don't go sunbathing on the beach at 2 o'clock in the morning. No, we do it when the sun is out to refresh and warm us. We don't plant new flowers in the backyard in November. We plant them when conditions are right for their proper growth. Sometimes, though, we neglect to use our own cycles to our advantage.

For example, I've discovered that I'm a morning person. I wake up eager to get the day's activities going. I play better golf in the morning than I do in the afternoon. I get more writing done if I attack the keyboard before noon. Others may prefer to sleep late and work in the afternoon hours or even at night. It's an individual preference or inclination that each person has to evaluate.

Once you discover your peak periods, you can then utilize them to the maximum. Do your creative work when you're traditionally the most enthused. If you're a morning person, work on your creative projects in the morning. It's that simple. You'll accomplish more and the quality will be better.

Now…what do you do with the rest of your day? Obviously, we can't spend all of our waking hours being creative. It would get monotonous and wearying. Besides, you need some activities to support your creative activities. For instance, if you're an artist, you have to buy supplies, go to the framing store, or research what painting you're going to begin next. Plan your non-creative, or supporting tasks, for when you're least enthusiastic. These *clerical* tasks require less energy and less creativity.

As a writer who prefers to work in the morning, it would be inefficient for me to spend those valuable hours writing letters, calling publishers, and doing research while I'm fresh and passionate, and then attacking the work that I really care about when I'm tired from doing all the *desk* work.

Conversely, a writer who prefers the evening hours would be better served by getting the clerical work out of the way while he's in his morning fog and saving the real work for his more energetic evening hours.

It's simply a way of making better use of your most energetic segments of your day.

6. Make Use of "Wait" Time in Your Activity:

Whichever activity you're working on, it will most likely have some periods of forced non-activity. If you're doing an oil painting, you may have to wait for the paint on one portion of the scene to dry before you can begin painting another facet. If you're working in carpentry, as we mentioned earlier, you may have to wait for the glue to set before you can again work on the piece.

There's nothing you can really do to speed up the drying of paint or glue, so what are your options? That's what you'll have to figure out. One option is to utilize the ideas we talked about in Item 3 of this list—plan your work so that you can easily find something to fill this *wait* time.

Another alternative is to work on several projects at the same time. While you're waiting for the glue to set on the bookcase you're building, you might be able to cut the pieces to size for the end table you've designing. While you're waiting for the paint to dry on your seascape, you might throw some paint onto a canvas for the still life you've planned.

Freelance writing is a good illustration of the value of this device. A writer might complete work on a novel, short story, or non-fiction article, then send it out to a buyer. It takes time for the editors to review the work and make a decision to either buy or reject it. It's wasting time for that writer to sit and wait for a reply. During the interim, the writer should be cranking out more pages—writing another novel, a short story, or a non-fiction article that she can send out to more publishers to generate more sales.

7. Divide Your Project into *Bite-size* Chunks:

No one can sit down and write a novel in one piece. No one can complete a masterpiece painting as one segment. No, the author writes words, pages, chapters, and all of this adds up to a novel. The artist paints background, eyes, ears, mouth, hair, in order to eventually complete a portrait. The whole is also made up of several parts.

I like to call these *bite-size* chunks. They're smaller segments of the entire project that you can attack when you have a few moments of spare time. Often an overall project can be intimidating and overwhelming. "Why should I work on that? I'll never get it completed." This thinking makes it easy, sometimes, to procrastinate.

However, if you've got small portions of the overall project laid out in your mind, you know you can complete one or two of those with relative ease. Your argument for putting the project off loses its impact.

Let me use this book as an example. I've included a chapter of 101 creative projects with a brief paragraph or two about each activity. Even if I didn't have time to concentrate on writing a chapter or even a few pages of a chapter, I could always sit at the keyboard and write a brief paragraph or two about one, two, or maybe even five of those creative projects.

I mentioned earlier a gentleman who was intent on learning a new language. He practiced using new vocabulary words as he took his daily walk. However, he also had those vocabulary words available as bite-size chunks that he could readily study. Even if he didn't want to get the textbooks out and study grammatical formations and do several translations, he could select five or ten vocabulary words and commit those to memory fairly easily.

In your planning under Item 3 in this list, try to include some of these bite-size chunks.

8. Engage in Your Creative Activity Whenever the Spirit Moves You:

Earlier, of course, I suggested that you plan an inflexible time for your creative work (Item 2, above). That's still a good idea, but it doesn't preclude you from working creatively anytime you feel the urge. If you feel that you'd like to work on your project right now, do it. By all means, do it. That's when you'll not only be most productive, but you'll probably have the most fun.

9. Convert Your Free Time to Productive Time:

Television work a few years ago was seasonal. A writer would work on a show for about thirty-six weeks and then have a sixteen-week hiatus. When I first began working as a TV writer, that forced vacation scared me. I asked my agent what I should do about it. He said, "Treat it like a government grant. Use this time to write a screen-play."

You can also do the same thing with any free time you have. It doesn't have to be a six-week hiatus. It can be a five- or ten-minute break from your other activities. It can be the last ten or fifteen minutes of your lunch break.

10. Prepare for "Wasted" Time:

The big complaint about jury duty is that you spend an entire day sitting in a room waiting to be called. Unless you're the type of person who can comfortably arrive at the airport just as they're closing the gates to the boarding ramp, you'll have to spend "wasted" time waiting to board. Very rarely will you arrive at the doctor's office for a 9 o'clock appointment and have the clerk open the door at 9 on the dot and say, "The doctor will see you now."

However, you can convert that "wasted" time to valuable minutes (or hours) to work on your creative activity. Wait a minute, though. Suppose you're doing a clay sculpture of a bunny rabbit. You can't take the clay and all your tools into the doctor's office and start working on the little bunny nose. You can't set up a studio in the jury waiting room. You're certainly not going to lug all that paraphernalia onto the plane as carry-on, either.

Nevertheless, there are ways that you can do some valuable research on whatever activity you're involved in. For example, you might bring along a book on sculpting that you can read while you're waiting for the judge, the doctor, or the aircraft.

You can do some of the planning that was discussed in Item 3 of this list.

Understand that these *time-altering* devices are not commandments. No one of them is a prerequisite for engaging in whatever creative activity you'd like to attempt. If you want to start building models of antique cars and you don't want to worry about plans or time schedules or working on it at a regularly scheduled time, go ahead and start building models whenever and however you want.

Whatever you choose should be an activity that you want to enjoy. Some of these suggestions might sound like we're converting this pastime into a job, an ordeal, or a sentence. No. These are simply devices for those who feel that they honestly don't have enough time to tackle a relaxing activity. Some of these devices may help those people find the time.

Understand, also, that these devices are illusions. We're not stretching time, bending time, creating time, or manipulating time. Time, as I've said earlier, is immutable. We're actually *tricking ourselves*. We're playing little parlor games with our minds to convince ourselves that we can use the limited amount of time that we do have more efficiently and effectively.

The point is that these techniques work. Once we get past the concept that we don't have enough time, we find that we have plenty of time to do those things that we really want to do.

Probably the most important time-saving device is to have fun with your project. Enjoy what you're doing and you'll discover that time will zoom by without your realizing it. This is the amazing aspect of any pursuit—time will cease to become a factor. It will feel like you have all the time you need.

So be creative and have fun.

[handwritten margin notes:] what's wrong w/ that? I love to work, work is play much of the time.

ok — agree but I also work

Chapter 8

Not Enough Money?

Money, unlike time, can be put to work to generate more money. It can be accumulated, saved up for a rainy day. If you need more, it's possible to earn more. Yet money in its own devilish way can be as much or more trouble to manipulate than time.

One problem is that money is not evenly distributed. We all get 24 hours in each day—no more, no less. Money is not so impartial. Some seem to have more than they need, while others of us never seem to have enough.

Some of the creative projects you want to explore may seem to you to be out of your price range. They may be a bit more costly than you prefer. However, with some ingenuity and perseverance, there may be ways to finance even expensive hobbies.

Let's look at a few of these ways:

1. Save for the Activity You Want to Pursue:

Let's assume that whatever activity you want to pursue has a price tag on it. It's going to cost you a certain amount. Let's assume further that you don't have those kinds of funds available. That doesn't mean you'll never have these funds available. Remember that cash, unlike time, can be accumulated. You can figure out what your costs will be and then figure out how much you can save. Then you can calculate when you'll have the necessary funds to begin.

Actually, this gives birth to another interesting creative activity—devising ways and implementing your plan to accumulate enough cash to get started on the project you want to undertake.

2. Earn the Money You'll Need:

Time, as we have noted, is forever fixed. That's not changeable. However, you *can* increase your cash flow. This may take a little planning and ingenuity, but you can earn the money you'll need for your creative activity by working at something else.

Maybe you take a part-time job. Perhaps you sell some of your services. Maybe you negotiate an increase in your current salary which can help earn the funds you'll need for your creative pursuit.

With some planning, some creativity, and much dedication, you should be able to find ways to finance your creative ambition.

3. "Steal" Funds from Other Activities:

One time my wife and I were preparing to go to work on a Friday morning. Friday happened to be payday for both of us. We were so low on funds that I had to ask my wife for carfare so I could get to work to pick up my paycheck. She said, "I was just about to ask you for carfare." Neither one of us had enough cash to get to work to pick up our salaries.

We had to find the money somewhere. My wife went into her closet and brought out all of her purses. We turned them upside down and salvaged enough loose change from them to pay our bus fares to work.

We "found" cash that had been forgotten about. However, you might be able to "find" cash in your own budget that can go toward financing your creative pursuit. For instance, you might eat out one less night a month and put that money towards funding your project. Perhaps you can cut out one magazine subscription. Maybe you can see one less movie or see the movie and skip the popcorn and soft drink. It's really up to your own particular circumstances and your own inventive cost reduction strategies.

I call this "stealing" from other activities. What it amounts to, simply, is more aggressive and inventive budgeting. It's budgeting with a purpose to finance your goal.

4. Redirect Some of Your Present Income to Your Creative Project:

Most books on financing advise "paying yourself first." What this means is that each person should set aside a percentage of his or her income for savings. In other words, if you earn $100 a day, take $10 off the top and put it into your savings account. Pay yourself first.

The premise is that if you take that money out of your income immediately, you won't really miss it. Thus, you'll be saving for your future *painlessly*.

You can use the same idea to fund whatever activity you want to engage in. Set aside a certain amount of time from your regular job, or a certain percentage of your regular income as financing for your creative activity.

If you work an eight-hour day, convince yourself that the money you earn in the last half-hour of each workday is assigned to your pastime. It's not too much of a financial burden but it may enable you to pursue your goal.

If you have a fixed income, maybe you can decide that a percentage of it is relegated to funding your project.

It's a mind trick, just like we played with time, but if it works for you, take advantage of it.

5. Make Whatever Activity You Select Pay for Itself:

I knew an ambitious gentleman who wanted to study to become a comedy writer. One writing course appealed to him, but it was a bit expensive for him at the time. However, he called several comics in his area who needed fresh material. He offered them an ingenious deal: "You pay for my comedy writing instruction and any homework I do as part of the course, I'll do with you in mind. Any material I create will be yours to use."

One comedian snapped up the deal. The writer took the course, the comic got the material, and it was a win-win situation for both.

How you might use this idea depends on what activity you're interested in, how it lends itself to this concept, and how creative you can be in finding ways to make your pursuit pay for itself. But it's an available option that shouldn't be overlooked.

6. Trade What You Have for What You Want:

Someone once explained that the real value of money is the services you receive for it. You accumulate funds so that you can trade them in for services. You take your salary and use it to purchase food for your table. You trade your money for the services that farmers and supermarkets provide. You fund your education with cash. You trade your money for the services that teachers and learning institutions offer you.

It's possible, though, that money doesn't even have to be involved in the transaction. You can trade services for services. I knew one gentleman who was beginning a career as a motivational speaker; however, he couldn't afford to open a representative office and hire clerical workers. He negotiated a deal by which he provided training for the employees of a well-established company. In return, he received office space and clerical help in this company's building.

There's a story that Johnny Carson once sold his home to a well-known tennis professional. Part of the sale price was that the tennis pro had to give Johnny Carson a series of tennis lessons.

As a person who has lived over fifty years, you have some expertise in various areas. Perhaps you can trade these skills for whatever services you need to begin your creative activity. "I'll teach you to read music if you'll give me a few art lessons." "I'll teach you to play bridge if you'll teach me how to crochet."

You finance your new creative activity and take cold, hard cash right out of the equation.

7. Turn Your Activity into a Profit-Making Endeavor:

Rather than thinking how you can pay for what you want to do, you can start thinking of how what you want to do can pay you for doing it. When I wanted to learn the craft of comedy writing, I bought a book on the subject which cost me about $4.95 at the time.

I read through the book, wrote a few one-liners, sent them to some of the markets suggested in the book, and got a check in the mail for twenty-five dollars. That wasn't a bad return on my investment.

If you're interested in cake decorating, you might be able to provide the cake for your company's annual Christmas party or some other event...for a fee.

If you want to study interior decorating, you might land a deal to offer some decorating advice for a friend's new home...for a fee.

Almost any creative project you select can have a profit making facet connected with it, provided you explore the possibilities and employ a bit of marketing and sales ingenuity.

Of course, this doesn't mean that you have to turn your creative hobby into a business. It can still be a pleasant diversion, but one that has enough profit attached to it to pay for itself.

8. Do a Little Bit Less:

Suppose you want to study oil painting and there is a well regarded studio near you that offers lessons. However, the weekly lessons are too expensive. They're twice what you want to pay. Well, then why not take half as many? Take a lesson every other week. This compromise effectively brings the weekly cost down to what you can afford.

9. Find a Cheaper Alternative:

Let's suppose you'd like to begin building models of famous ships like the *HMS Bounty* or the *USS Constitution*. You do some research and discover that the cost of these kits can run from $200 to $700. That may be a bit more than you wanted to pay. However, you might be able to find good challenging models of whaling boats or rowboats that cost considerably less. There are also simple models that may be less intricate, yet just as rewarding, that may only cost around $25 or $30. This way you can begin the hobby, have some fun with it, and keep it within budget. You can also gain some experience and expertise working on these less challenging models while you're saving some money to indulge in the more expensive versions.

Maybe you enjoy oil painting and giving your productions to friends. However, framing each picture is expensive. You might paint around the edges of the canvas, so that the picture can be presented unframed. Or, since you're painting anyway, you might paint the frame right onto the canvas. Mix a little faux painting into your scene to cut down on costs.

Suppose you want to take some lessons—golf, tennis, or ballroom dancing—but the cost is prohibitive. You might be able to get those same lessons at a much cheaper rate by signing up for group lessons. Perhaps you can assemble your own group and negotiate with the teachers for a less expensive group rate.

* * *

These, of course, are not the only ways to solve the "money problem." You may have some ingenious plans of your own. Fine. Make use of them.

The point here is that money often is more of a convenient excuse than a valid obstacle. With ingenuity, perseverance, and devotion, money problems can usually be resolved.

Chapter 9

What to Do? What to Do?

The first step in pursuing a creative activity is deciding on which creative activity to pursue. If you've already decided on a creative project, congratulations. You can proceed to the next chapter…BUT WAIT!

Maybe you should read through this chapter anyway. It might inspire you to try a few other activities. Or it may present some intriguing ideas that you've never considered.

* * *

If you haven't decided on a creative endeavor, the thoughts and suggestions presented in this chapter will help guide your thinking.

Below are twelve areas that can help you organize your research. Focus on these specific areas, one at a time, and jot down any activities that interest you. These are brain-storming tools, so disregard any negative ideas. For instance, don't reject an idea because it might be too expensive, or too complicated, or because you might not have the necessary skills. All of that logical thinking, fine tuning, and prioritizing will come later. For now, the important objective is to gather ideas. Therefore, without being too critical, list any activities that have potential.

1. Recall Your Childhood Dreams:

In the earlier chapters we discussed those fantasies and goals you had as a youngster. Then Life happened while you were busy making other plans. You may have abandoned, replaced, ignored, or forgotten about many of them. However, some of them may simply be repressed. Now is a good time to recall them, jot a few of them down, and make them part of your research.

2. Consider any Skills You Once Had but May Have Neglected:

During our young adult years, we devoted much of our energy, concentration, and effort towards finding our vocation and making a living from it. Several of the fun activities that interested us may have been sacrificed to maximize our earnings. You may have been pretty good at some of those things you had to abandon. And, in fact, you may still be pretty good at them.

Consider some of those skills you had. Maybe you were a pretty good columnist for the school paper and even considered a writing career. You may have had a fine eye for decorating. Perhaps friends were always amazed at how skilled you were at drawing. Maybe you showed promise as a musician until the lessons became too costly or the practice hours too inconvenient.

Spend a bit of time thinking back on your earlier talents. Jot them down on this comprehensive list. One of them may be the creative activity you'll pursue once again.

3. Think About those Many Things You Always Wanted to Try but Never Got Around to:

Surely you can think of a few in this category. Some of them may be a bit bizarre, even scary. Nevertheless, include even those in your list. Why? Because some of those unattainable goals may turn out now to actually be attainable. Even if they're not, putting them on your list could trigger interesting creative activities that might be associated with them. For instance, you may have no hope of becoming the bull rider that you hoped you would be, but you might do some interesting paintings or drawings of bull riding.

So, think of endeavors you wish you had tried, but never did. Make them part of your *shopping list*.

4. Note General Areas that You're Interested In:

All of us have topics that we're not essentially connected to, but that we're fascinated with. One friend of mine is a Civil War buff. He reads everything he can about that period of history—the battles and the military strategy connected with them. Another friend is just as intrigued by World War II. Me, I was always intrigued by stage magic. I used to collect how-to books on sleight of hand, not so much so that I could practice and perfect the skills, but so that I could be aware of some of the moves and try to figure out just how certain performers accomplished their amazing feats.

Interests can range anywhere from airplanes to zoology, including all the letters of the alphabet in between. By including your unique interests in this list you should be able to find some interesting activity connected to it.

5. Include Some Areas that You'd Like to Learn About:

At a party once, a group of us adults were having some fun with a child's toy called "Etch-a-Sketch." It's a small silver screen with two knobs at the bottom. One knob moves a marker up and down and the other moves the marker left to right. As you manipulate these two controls, you direct a line that is being *etched* onto the silver screen.

All of us took some turns creating weird, wacky, funny designs. Each one of us tried to be more creative and funnier than the previous artist.

When we set the toy aside, one person picked up the toy and fiddled with it. He didn't draw designs. He held the device upside down, turned the knobs, and stared intently as the line formed on the screen. He was trying to discover how the mechanism inside this plaything operated.

I've toyed with an Etch-a-Sketch many times, and you probably have, too. But I have no idea how that line is formed on the screen. Honestly, I don't really care. But this gentleman did. He wanted to learn what made it work.

I mentioned earlier that while visiting Italy, I saw many of Michelangelo's masterpieces in marble—David, the Pietà, Moses and several others. They were inspiring statues. However, I wondered—did Michelangelo just grab a chisel and a hammer and start chipping away at a block of marble? How did he plan his work? What did he do if he made a slight misstep and chipped out a chunk of rock that shouldn't have been chipped out? How did he polish the finished piece to so fine a luster?

These things piqued my interest. So when I saw a class being offered in sculpting at a nearby adult school, I signed up. I still don't know what process Michelangelo used, but I do know a little bit about molding and forming clay and how to convert the finished clay model to a bronze piece.

Here's another aspect of engaging in a creative activity—it leads along many roads. Others in my clay sculpting class have carved in marble before. I'm sure they can give me some insights into the process. In this chain of learning, it's interesting how discovering one fact usually leads to another.

What you're curious about might lead to an interesting and creative pastime.

6. Consider Skills that Other People Say You Have:

Occasionally, the golf gods will smile on my game and I'll hit a superb shot—maybe about every three months or so. When I do, I usually say to the guy riding in the golf cart with me, with as much fake sincerity as I can muster, "Honestly, I had no idea I was that good."

That's playful banter, of course, but sometimes it can be closer to the truth than we realize. (Not about my golf, certainly, but for other people in other areas.) It's quite possible that acquaintances may see in us a potential that we overlook in ourselves. With some reflection, you'll be able to recall certain compliments you've received repeatedly. "You have a good eye for color." "You're an excellent, entertaining speaker." "You have a very analytical mind." Whatever the compliments are, it would be wise to note them in this list. They might provide a clue to a creative activity that would not only interest you, but that you could excel at.

7. Think of Some Good You Would Like to Contribute:

Your creative activity may be helping other people to fulfill some of their dreams. It might be teaching nine-and ten-year-olds the fundamentals of baseball. It might be tutoring grade school students in math or English. It might be teaching art to underprivileged children or helping business executives polish their speaking skills.

Surely, you can find some areas in the world, or simply in your own community, that you would like to improve. These may trigger some suggestions for creative activities that will not only interest you, but also benefit others.

You needn't be an *expert* at what you do.

There's a story told about two campers enjoying a vacation in the wilds. A hungry bear threatens them. One camper starts changing into his running shoes. The other says, "Why are you doing that? You're never going to outrun a hungry bear." The camper replies, "I don't have to. I just have to outrun you."

That's the same idea with creative projects that educate others. You don't have to be a recognized authority; you simply have to have more information or skills than the people you're offering it to. It's not necessary to be an ex-major league ballplayer to coach tee ball in your community. You don't have to be a best-selling author to help youngsters who are having trouble with English.

Think of areas where you *want to help*; that may be the creative project you should begin.

8. Evaluate Activities that Could Benefit You Physically, Mentally, or in Any Way:

The doc says you should get a bit more exercise. Your spouse tells you losing a few pounds might not be a bad idea. Your boss tells you that your report writing could stand some fine tuning. You tell yourself that you probably should do some mental exercises to keep your mind sharp and your memory quick and reliable.

Make a list of those areas where you need work. Once you discover these, you can usually find creative activities that will accomplish the improvement for you. For instance, the boss wants your report writing to improve; so, take a course in writing informative magazine articles. Sign up for a correspondence course or an Internet workshop, or attend classes at an adult education center. The writing you do in connection with any project will enhance your report writing. Both you and your boss will be happier.

9. Focus on Self-improvement:

Benjamin Franklin's autobiography is a classic example of beginning a creative program of self-improvement. Franklin made a list of areas that he wanted to correct. He then devised a scorecard and kept accurate records of the progress he made toward each goal.

You don't need the detail and determination of Franklin. All you have to do for your research is think of some skills that you would like to acquire for you own satisfaction and self-improvement.

For instance, if you would like to improve your ability to concentrate, maybe you could pick up a book of interesting logic problems or puzzles and begin solving them. If you want to improve some personal trait, perhaps you could begin keeping a journal each day of what specifically you're doing and how you're progressing.

With some research and ingenuity you can find projects that will contribute to your own devotion to self-improvement.

If you want to learn humility, take up golf.

10. Start a New Business:

There's nothing wrong with making your creative pursuit an active business venture. Colonel Sanders, of KFC fame, was sixty-five years old when he began franchising his Kentucky Fried Chicken outlets. Within ten years he had over 600 franchises in operation.

Of course, your business venture doesn't have to have the scope and the profitability of the KFC empire. Your business might be a simple operation that generates a few bucks each week. It's not the size of the venture that makes it appealing; it's the fun and the satisfaction of running a successful business venture—whether it's for multi-millions or snack money.

If there's a business you'd like to initiate, promote, and make a profit from, doing so could settle your creative involvement for some time.

11. Consider Your Legacy:

How do you want to be remembered? What do you want to be remembered for? Are there things you'd like to leave for your children? If so, there are certain things that must be done now so they won't be forgotten in the future.

This must have happened to you—you rummage through some old photographs. You find one of several old and dear friends. You're all obviously having a wonderfully good time together. However, you can't recall who half of them are. "Is that Uncle John or is it Charlie McNally who lived down the street?" "I know this guy and this girl, but I have no idea who that is."

Maybe a worthwhile creative activity would be to begin a scrapbooking process of your own family photos. Label them all so that when you or your relatives pick them up years from now, you'll know exactly who Uncle John is.

Or you might begin writing your memoirs and having them bound for close friends and relatives. Once your story is on paper, it's hard to forget.

A friend of mine memorialized her family's favorite recipes by interviewing relatives. She produced a book of everyone's favorite meals, including the recipes and some tales that went with each one. She also included pictures and labeled them.

This family now not only knows who Uncle John was, but what his favorite dish was, along with Aunt Sally's recommendations for preparing it.

12. Just to Prove that You Can:

Let's say you never learned to play the piano. Every time your wife asks you to dance you find an excuse not to. Why? Because you never learned to dance properly. Your older sister was a pretty good artist and everyone of your relatives has a painting of hers hanging somewhere in their house. However, you never bothered with art.

Now, you may want to prove that you can do these things. You may want to prove that you can do other things, too.

Jot down those things you want to do now just to prove that you can do them. Add these to your list of potential activities.

By now, you should have an exhaustive, almost overwhelming, list of potential projects. The next challenge is to boil them down to the one project—or maybe the top five or ten—you want to begin now. You can do this with a series of eliminations.

You have a list which is in no particular order. In order to determine the one you truly want to begin, compare the first two projects on your list. Assume that you can only select one. Which one of these two would you choose?

OK, now eliminate the other one.

Take the remaining project and compare it with the next one on the list. Which of these two would you prefer. Cross out the rejected one.

Repeat this selection process, pair by pair, until you have only one item remaining. This is the creative activity you've chosen to attack first.

In order to clarify the selection procedure, let's go through a short, hypothetical list, where the hypothetical me has selected one project from each of the twelve focus points listed above.

From (1) Childhood Dreams, I've chosen taking singing lessons. I always had fantasies about being a recording star. At least now I can learn to sing properly. Can I afford the lessons? Can I find a competent teacher nearby? Do I have the necessary talent? Will it serve my purposes? None of that really matters at this point. This is only research and brainstorming. So "singing lessons" goes on my list.

From (2) Neglected Skills, I'm opting for learning to play golf. I was always fairly competent at sports and played golf for a while many years ago. Maybe now is the time to take the game up more seriously.

Under (3) Things I Wanted to Do but Never Got Around To, I'm jotting down becoming an actor. That art form always fascinated me. It seems like fun and I feel I might be competent. So maybe I'll audition for some roles, either professionally or in local theater groups. Acting goes on my list.

From (4) General Areas of Interest, I'm listing studying psychology in college. That science has always fascinated me, so maybe it could be a new pursuit for me.

Under (5) Things to Learn About, my selection is sculpting. I don't know much about it, but would like to learn. I may not have the skill for it, but I suppose I'll find out quickly enough. "Take a sculpting class" goes on my list.

Under (6) Skills That Other People Say I Have, I'm listing short story writing. Folks always say I have a way of making a story sound interesting. Maybe I should learn how to organize my stories, commit them to paper, and perhaps sell them to magazines.

From (7) Good Things I'd Like to Do, I've chosen helping out as a Little League coach. I've always enjoyed watching youngsters playing baseball, but feel I might be able to help them to learn the fundamentals. I'm sure any league would welcome some adult help, so that goes on my *shopping list.*

Under (8) Activities That Could Benefit Me Physically, Mentally, or in any Way, I noted that I could use a more regular, intensive exercise program, so my activity would be to organize some interesting hikes…and then stick to the schedule.

From (9) Self-Improvement, I've decided to study French. I've always wanted to learn a second language, so that'll be one of my potential activities.

Under (10) Begin a New Business, the speaking profession appeals to me. I enjoy writing speeches and talking in front of people. I enjoy the laughter and the applause. I've always been successful at entertaining at work and social functions, so maybe I can turn speaking into a profitable profession.

From (11) What Is My Legacy, I've jotted down "writing my memoirs." I've had some interesting adventures, some intriguing tales to tell. Now is the time to get them on paper.

From (12) Just to Prove I Can, I've listed "learning to play the piano." I should have done it when I was young, but I didn't. There's no real reason why I can't study and learn it now.

So, my list looks like this:

- Take singing lessons
- Learn to play golf
- Become an actor

- Take a college course in psychology
- Attend sculpting lessons
- Write short stories
- Help coach in Little League
- Begin a hiking regimen
- Learn to speak French
- Become a public speaker
- Write my memoirs
- Learn to play the piano

Next, I'll go through the pair-by-pair elimination process.

First, would I rather take singing lessons or play golf? I've opted for learning golf. The singing lessons are eliminated for now.

Now, I choose between playing golf and becoming an actor. Golf is fun, but acting seems like more of a challenge. I'll eliminate golf.

Now, I must compare acting to taking a college course in psychology. Acting is sort of like learning psychology anyway, so I'll choose acting again. The psychology studies are rejected.

Now, I must choose between acting and sculpting. Tough choice here, but I'm going with sculpting. Acting is abandoned at this time.

The decision now is between sculpting and writing short stories. Once again, I'm staying with the sculpting lessons.

Next, I must select either sculpting or coaching Little League. I'll stick with sculpting. My coaching career is postponed.

Now, the choice is either sculpting or a hiking program. I'll stay with sculpting once again. Hiking is ruled out.

Now, the decision is to do the sculpting or to learn to speak French. This is a close one, but I'm opting once again for the sculpting.

Now, do I stick with sculpting or begin to look for opportunities to become a speaker? I'll stick with sculpting.

Now, it's a choice between sculpting and writing my memoirs. I'd love to learn sculpting (and I may later) but for now I think writing my memoirs is important. I cross out the sculpting lessons.

Finally, do I elect to write my memoirs or learn to play piano? Again, it's toss-up, but I think for now, my memoirs win out.

So, the last project standing is "writing my memoirs."

By making a list of possible projects and then eliminating them one by one, I've decided that I'll begin the creative process of researching, organizing, writing, and publishing my memoirs.

* * *

This doesn't mean that all the other interesting projects should be ignored. You can probably support several creative projects at one time. Memoir writing is the top priority for now, but I can go through the same elimination process with the ones that were rejected.

I may discover that I want to take those sculpting classes anyway. I can take those on Monday and Wednesday mornings and still get a good chunk of my life story on paper during the rest of the week.

Going through the process once again, I may decide that I want to try out for a role in the next production at the Community Players.

Who knows? Maybe the hypothetical me will become a star, have my memoirs already prepared for mass publication, and do a bronze bust of myself for the Acting Hall of Fame. That's a lot of accomplishments for a guy who also coaches Little League.

* * *

So that's my hypothetical selection process. Now you can get busy making your own choices. Once you decide what to do…what to do…we'll discuss how to go about getting started doing it.

Chapter 10

One-Time Projects

Several years ago, the tennis club I belonged to offered a series of lessons for youngsters. My grandson, who was around five years old at the time, took the classes. After he attended a few sessions, I asked him if he enjoyed taking the lessons. He said, "I wouldn't want to do it for the rest of my life."

That may be the way some of you are feeling about these creative projects about now. "They sound like fun, but I wouldn't want to do them for the rest of my life." Good news—not every one of these adventures requires a lifetime commitment. Some of them can simply be a "let's do it and get it over with" kind of deal. It's acceptable to consider some of these activities as a one-time project.

Have you ever tried to do a watercolor, oil, or acrylic painting? Why not do one now? How about acting in a play or working backstage at a local theater production. If you've never tried it before, it might be an interesting experience. Maybe you could build a dollhouse for your granddaughter. (Of course, if you have several granddaughters, this could turn into a lifetime commitment.) Everyone has a secret desire to write. You could determine to complete a short story. Heck, maybe even write a novel or a screenplay if you're really ambitious.

A golfing buddy of mine recently sold his business so that he could retire comfortably. However, to fill his leisure hours he decided to begin a novel. "In my business, I always had to write proposals and reports," he said. "I know how to write, so I thought it might be fun to at least get started on a fictional book." Within the space of a year and a half, he had completed and published three novels—a trilogy about country club politics. Now that they're on the bookstore shelves, he's completed a fourth manuscript on a totally different topic.

Why a one-time project?

1. For a Specific Purpose:

You may want to create something unique for a special event. For instance, if you want to present an original gift to friends who are celebrating a special anniversary, you could "publish" a book of humorous memories. This could be a series of photographs you have of them, with humorous captions. Or you could collect funny pictures from magazines and newspapers and write witty remarks that have special meaning for your friends. Maybe you could simply assemble a scrapbook commemorating this special occasion.

You might want to provide a cake that is decorated "personally" by you for them. By "personally," I mean the cake may be made in the shape of a catcher's mitt if they're big baseball fans. It could have a school insignia as a decoration if they happened to have met at a certain university. The cake could even feature a scene of an "inside joke" that has special meaning only to them and their friends. It'll be appreciated much more than the traditional, "Happy Anniversary, Harry and Sally."

It could be that you need something for the house—a piece of furniture, a special painting for a certain spot on the wall, maybe some faux painting for the wall above the fireplace. It might be the reason you need to try something creative—just for this one application.

Or, maybe you do want to build a dollhouse for your granddaughter's Christmas present.

A friend of mine was celebrating a round-numbered anniversary and he insisted that the children not spend a lot of money for gifts. He requested that they offer only presents that they made. So on the evening of the celebration, all the children came in with a large, gift-wrapped package. When the anniversary couple received the gift, they noticed that it felt a little warm to the touch. They removed the wrapping to reveal a large bake pan of freshly cooked lasagna. The kids had *made* dinner and that was their gift.

It's nice to be clever and creative.

2. As a Challenge:

Why do we work crossword puzzles and figure out which number goes where in a sudoku block? Because we want to test ourselves. We want to outsmart the puzzle. Why do we play golf? We want to test our skills against the various courses, weather conditions, and so on. Creative people enjoy a challenge. They're eager to prove to themselves that they can do something.

Have you ever done a wood carving of a giraffe? Do you think you would like to try? Do you have a good reason to try? Then try it.

3. Just to Have Done it:

So you've never cross-stitched a pillow that says, "I smile because I'm your sister. I laugh because there's nothing you can do about it." But you've always wanted to cross-stitch a pillow that says, "I smile because I'm your sister. I laugh because there's nothing you can do about it," and present it as a birthday gift to your younger sister.

So what do you do? You cross-stitch a pillow that says, "I smile because I'm your sister. I laugh because there's nothing you can do about it." There, now you've done it. Now you can say to yourself, "I've finally cross-stitched a pillow that says, 'I smile because I'm your sister. I laugh because there's nothing you can do about it.'"

Isn't that a nice feeling?

4. Just for the Fun and Relaxation:

Whatever one-time project you're initiating should be for your enjoyment as much as any other reason. It's something that's waiting for your attention when you have nothing else to do and would like to occupy your mind and your skills on *something*.

You might even make a list of projects that you can work on when the spirit moves you. It's like a "to-do" list. Once I wanted to make a "to-do" list of household chores that I had been meaning to complete, but never had. My wife volunteered to get the list started for me. She wrote on there, "Item 1—Do items 2, 3, 4, 5, and 6 NOW!"

You don't have to be quite so authoritarian with yourself. But having a list of things you might want to try when you get the time could come in handy when you do find out that you have the time.

There are several benefits to these one-time creative projects.

First of all, you'll have the finished product. If you needed a picture for a bare spot on the wall and you complete a lovely snow scene, mission accomplished. If you needed a memorable gift for friends and you complete a book of photographs with personalized, humorous captions, wrap it up and take it to the party. You may never build another dollhouse, but your efforts will be rewarded when you see your granddaughter's eyes light up on Christmas morning.

Second, you'll enjoy the pride of accomplishment. It's very satisfying to succeed at something you've never tried before. Pat yourself on the back, brag to your friends, relish your success.

Third, you'll not only gain some knowledge about the activity you've tried, but you'll gain an appreciation for a skill that you never had before. Once you attempt something, you learn how difficult it can be, and you'll gain a new insight into that art or craft. You'll have a new reverence for the experts in that field.

Fourth, you'll have resolved a craving. There's a nagging element to having something you would like to attempt, but never attempted. It's an empty, unsatisfying feeling. It's like having a knife full of peanut butter, but with nothing to spread it on. Doing what you've wanted to do satisfies that feeling. You can say to yourself, "OK, I've done it. I may never do it again (and maybe you didn't do it very well), but at least I've done it."

The parenthetical part in the previous paragraph is important. It's not required that you do this project well. If it doesn't turn out well, you can tear it up, or chop it up, or burn it, or bury it. It's not important. What counts is that you tried it. You did it.

Fifth (the phrase "last but not least" certainly applies here because this might be the most important benefit of all), you might discover that you like it. You might surprise yourself and discover that you're not only good at what you attempted, but you thoroughly enjoy the activity. It may turn out to be "a keeper."

Unlike my grandson's tennis lessons, you may want to pursue this for the rest of your life.

Chapter 11

101 Creative Activities

As a comedy writing instructor, I would often hand out an assignment for the students that entailed writing 101 jokes of a specific format. I discovered that writers not only enjoyed the challenge, but the assignment of a specific number of gags prompted them to write more material than they thought they could. It showed them that they had more humorous thoughts on the subject than they ever imagined they could have.

Following are 101 creative activities. This list is by no means exhaustive and the particular activity you're interested in may not be listed. The purpose here is to show you that there are fascinating and challenging creative activities available to you. If nothing here appeals to you, I'm sure you can find something that does suit your interests.

Besides, making this list was an interesting creative activity for me.

So here they are in alphabetical order.

Acting—Professional or Semi-Professional:

When I was writing scripts, it never seemed to me that acting was that creative. You just say the words that are written on the page. The real creative process was in thinking up the words to put on that page.

I'm kidding, of course (kind of). Some pieces I wrote played beautifully in one performance and terribly in another. The difference was in the skill and creativity of the different performers.

It takes considerable vision to read into the words on a page and extract the character. Then it takes ingenuity to find a way to portray that character to the audience. It's not as easy as the great thespians make it appear. Like many other skills, when it's done well, it looks easy.

Acting can be great fun, too. Acting gives you the opportunity to be various people with different characteristics and personalities. It's a chance to get out of yourself and become a fictional character.

There's money to be made in the acting profession, too—both professionally and semi-professionally.

Antique Hunting:

This involves finding and visiting places where antiques might be available—garage sales, estate sales, interesting shops in out-of-the-way places. Discovering those places is an adventure in itself.

Much of the creativity, though, comes from learning about whatever type of antiques you're shopping for. That's the only way to know when you've found something authentic and perhaps valuable.

This can certainly be a money making venture if you are knowledgeable, but on the other hand, it can simply be an interesting way of discovering treasures that are beautiful and perhaps valuable only to you.

Baking:

Cakes, pies, breads—whatever. You can always add some *secret* ingredients to traditional recipes or even invent some delicious concoctions of your own. There's always the creativity, too, of adding your own personal touches to the process.

The results of this activity are always appreciated by someone.

Ballet:

It's not too late.

Ballroom Dancing:

This is a wonderful activity that both you and your spouse will appreciate. It's not only great fun and exercise, but it's a magnificent boost to the ego. Being able to step onto the dance floor and look smooth and graceful always gives you a warm glow of self-satisfaction. Once you learn the basic steps, your creativity will probably prod you into adding a few dazzling moves of your own, or at least a flourish or two that makes you and your partner look even more graceful.

There may be some fringe benefits involved, too. When my wife and I took lessons a few years ago, we enjoyed dancing so much that we signed on for a few cruises because onboard the ship, we could dance practically every night.

Bird Watching:

Here you can learn to identify different species of birds by their appearance, their call, or sometimes simply the distinctive way they fly through the air. This activity requires a little bit of study and skill, along with patience. People who practice this hobby can be thrilled both at how many different species they can record and when they spot a type of bird that rarely appears in their area.

Bird watching also gets you out walking, which is good exercise.

Blogging:

We hear this term more and more lately. It seems to be a major force in the communication business. I honestly don't know much about it. It involves computers, websites, and such. However, it's popular and powerful, and is most likely a quite creative endeavor.

Cake Decorating (Fondant):

Fondant is a mixture of sugar and water that can be formed into a thin, sheet-like layer used to cover cakes. You can add food coloring to produce different hues and either paint or carve pictures into your cake.

You can learn to make your own fondant, buy mixes, or even buy the fondant ready-made. What you do with it after that is up to your own imagination.

Producers even market sheets of icing that are layered on a plastic covering and can be run through a special digital printing machine. Using these products, you can download pictures from the Internet or scan and print your own personal photos onto your cakes.

It's a fascinating, creative, useful art form. A quick search on the Internet will offer plenty of tips on the materials you'll need, where to get them, and also several sources of instruction.

Have fun with it, and save a slice for me.

Cake Decorating (Traditional):

This is the kind of decorating we're more used to—the pretty flowers and borders of icing on special event cakes. Generally, the effects are accomplished by squeezing icing out of the tube. It's a relatively simple process, but the resulting decorations can be astounding.

Again, a visit to the Internet will certainly list several sources of instructions.

Calligraphy:

This is a fancy word for fancy writing. We used to call it Old English, or Script, but there are all sorts of alphabets that you can use. There are several types of pens of varying sizes that are used for this form of art. As you become skilled with the manipulations of the pens, you will probably invent a few alphabets of your own.

It's fun to learn and a practical talent.

Candle Making:

A little bit of wax, some coloring agents, a wick in the middle, a touch of dexterity, and creativity and you'll wind up with some beautiful pieces of art that not only look appealing, but can smell nice, too.

Just like with the fondant, you can also embed photographs into the candles. Your resulting artwork makes appealing gifts for friends and desirable items for sale.

Candy Making:

What a delicious hobby this could be. It's a very delicate procedure in which temperatures and cooking time are critical. However, that makes it all the more challenging and interesting. Part of the fun would be in finding and cataloguing various tasty recipes. Another part of the fun would be in chomping on your products once they're completed.

You can be certain friends and acquaintances will be eager to get on your gift list if you perfect this craft.

Career Coach:

This can be a very rewarding and profitable activity. Now that you've lived for forty-nine years or more, you're probably qualified to offer some wise and beneficial advice to others.

There are classes that teach career coaching techniques. You can find these with a little bit of research. Then, marketing this talent and service is another good use for your creative talents.

Or, you can just offer your services in your field of expertise as a non-profit venture. It could be your way of giving back to the profession that you enjoyed.

Carpentry:

Not much has to be said about this craft. We all know what it is. But with some training, some dexterity, and some creativity, you can make some beautiful pieces for your own home, for friends, or for sale.

I watch Norm Abrams, the woodworker who has a show called "The New Yankee Workshop" on TV. I'm amazed that whenever he needs to do something—drill a hole, or carve a piece in a certain shape, or cut two pieces to fit together perfectly—he has a special tool designed specifically to do that. It's always a tool that I've never heard of and never knew existed.

On his website, newyankee.com, he offers detailed plans for many different projects, instructional videos, books, and lots of other stuff related to carpentry.

Caution, though—he's so good that he makes things look easy. They'll probably be more demanding for you and me...but they still look like fun to try.

Clown:

Didn't all of us love clowns at the circus, in parades, at parties? Didn't a lot of us fantasize about joining the circus? Maybe doing acrobatics on a high trapeze with no net below us was a bit too daring. Certainly being locked in a cage full of lions and tigers was too reckless. All of us, though, could be clowns.

It's not too late. I'm sure there are clown schools somewhere near where you live. In fact, there is an organization called Clowns of America International which has local chapters. Its website (coai.org) offers classes in various facets of being a clown.

Designing a creative outfit and your individual clown makeup would be part of this activity. Then you could market your entertaining services or simply offer them for parties and festivities at children's hospitals or countless other worthy functions.

Get a few laughs; it's fun.

Coin Collecting:

We all know about this hobby, but maybe not as much as we should. There are various facets to this activity. For instance, what type of coins you collect, from what era, from which countries, and so on.

The creativity comes in the research of discovering the specific coins you're interested in, where to find them, and, of course, determining how to afford to add them to your collection.

Collecting (anything and/or everything):

People collect anything—from airplane models to zebras. The creative effort here is in discovering something that you feel is worth collecting. Since I'm a writer, I'm interested in collecting miniature typewriters. A pilot friend of mine has a roomful of models of military aircraft. Another friend has a closet full of golfing hats from various locations. There's absolutely no limit to what you might want to start collecting.

Then you must work your imagination and research skills to find out where you might search for, whatever it is you're collecting. Even more inventiveness is involved in devising an attractive way of displaying your collection.

Of course, the most creativity is required in letting your friends and family know about your hobby and dropping effective, but subtle hints, so that they'll remember your interest at gift-giving times.

Colored Pencil Drawing:

An artist once showed me some of his work. It was exquisitely detailed and beautifully rendered portraiture. I asked how it was done. He said, "Colored pencils." It's amazing the dramatic effects one can achieve with these simple tools.

It's inexpensive, clean, and very effective. Another nice thing is that with today's technology, you don't even have to be an artist. You can print out photos on your computer and use a light board to trace out whatever picture you want to capture. The fun and creativity is in blending the colors to create a pleasing piece of art.

Community Theater—Acting:

We've already discussed the craft of acting. However, it needn't be undertaken for money. There are small theaters in nearly every community and they are always looking for people who want to get on stage and show off their skills.

Heck, it doesn't even have to be as organized as Community Theater. You can cast yourself for a part in skits that your church or organization may produce. The fun is in learning your script, being involved with the rest of the cast and crew, getting up there and showing off a bit, then accepting the applause from the audience. You might even get a bouquet of flowers after the last performance. It can be fun.

Community Theater—Set Designing:

"No way I'm walking onstage and making a fool of myself." Okay…if that's how you feel about acting, you can still be a part of local productions.

When the actors do walk on stage, they have to be somewhere— in a house, in a field—somewhere. You can get involved in painting the scenery or designing and decorating the sets. It's creative, it's fun, and it's Show Biz.

Community Theater—Stage Hand:

Okay…you can't act and you have no painting or designing skills. You can still be a part of local Show Biz. Any production, no matter how small or non-professional, needs people hustling around backstage, making the actors and the production look good. You can grab a hammer and some nails and help build the sets that the folks from the paragraph above have designed. You can work with the sound or the lighting. You can be the frantic person behind the scenery who helps the performers quickly change from one costume to another. There are countless chores you can do to live up to the age-old adage, "The show must go on." You may find it much more hectic than you figured, but it can still be fun.

Computer Art:

The standard excuse of non-artists is "I can't even draw a straight line." That rationalization never was valid because most artists can't draw a straight line either. However, it's even less acceptable today because you can get computers to generate your straight lines for you. In fact, you can get computers to do much of your art work today if you do the research and supply the creativity.

A quick search of "computer art" on the Internet provides lots of insight into the many different forms of this activity.

I looked the term up on Wikipedia and it says, "Computer art is any art in which computers play a role in the production or display of the artwork." I followed a few of the references and discovered that there is such a thing as digital painting. You can create beautiful landscapes or portraits using keystrokes instead of brush strokes. You can create abstract art, patterns, and lots of other intriguing artwork.

For some of these projects you may need to obtain some computer art software, but a quick search on the Internet will suggest a few of these, also.

Cooking:

A business associate of mine got hooked on several television cooking shows. He'd watch them religiously and was not only tempted by some of the delicious recipes, but was also enticed by the art of cooking. He was so intrigued, he took a few classes and became a gourmet chef.

Fine cooking is not only a skill, it can be a creative art form, too.

Cooking can be not only a pleasant pastime, but a delicious one, too.

Creating Theme Gift Baskets:

Recently I attended a fundraiser for Guide Dogs of America. The event featured a silent auction. Many of the auction items were attractive gift baskets, designed not only for dog lovers, but also for the dogs. Some of these were collections of chew toys and rawhide bones. Others were packages of various snacks for "Fido." A few of the baskets were sundry knick-knacks that would appeal to dog lovers—pillows with cute sayings, statues, clocks, whatever.

Finding items of specific interest, arranging them, and wrapping them attractively is a skill that can be enjoyed and beneficial. The end product can be used as sale items or silent auction items at fund raisers like the Guide Dogs of America event, or they make very appealing and appreciated gifts for special friends on special occasions.

Crocheting:

There's no end to the beautiful bric-a-brac you can generate with hands that are skillful at crocheting. Some families boast hand-crocheted tablecloths that have been passed down from generation to generation. You can make fancy coasters and decorative thingamabobs that go under plants and stuff around the house. My mom and sisters used to buy fancy colored thread and crochet decorative borders around ladies' handkerchiefs. They made welcome gifts.

There are books loaded with instructions for creating thousands of different items you can produce with good crocheting skills.

Cross-stitching:

This is practically an art form. Some of the pieces you can generate using this technique look almost like delicate paintings. It requires a steady hand, a good eye, and lots of patience, but it can be an interesting and highly artistic creative activity.

Decoupage:

This skill simply means to cut out pictures or documents, paste them together in an interesting assemblage, and then coat the finished product with a protective coating of some sort. You can create frameable pieces of art, decorate furniture, or rejuvenate antiques. You can apply this skill in countless ways.

A brief visit to the Internet or the library and you'll find easy-to-follow instructions, resources for the supplies you'll need, and tons of fun, practical projects to work on.

Designing:

This is admittedly a vague area. There are so many facets to designing. However, if you have a skill for creating interesting arrangements, you can pick and choose whichever facet of designing appeals to you. You might want to design fashions for men or women. You might like to lay out beautiful landscaping for gardens. Perhaps creating interesting office or home arrangements would appeal to you.

Digital Photo Albums:

It's always nice to pick up an album of family pictures and relive old memories. Nowadays, you can gather your photo collection into various albums by using your computer. There are software packages that help you catalogue your pictures and also arrange them into various albums. You might want to arrange them in logical collections, or you could create very attractive albums that you can print out for collection and storage.

Directing/Editing Short Videos:

Video cameras have become almost a standard family appliance nowadays. If you doubt this, go to any student recital at your local elementary school. One quarter of the people are seated quietly and the other 75 percent are standing at the front videotaping their child, grandchild, or great-grandchild.

You can begin producing, directing, and editing your own short videos. There's a free market for creative artistry in this field on the Internet, for example on YouTube. Also, you might submit your short pieces to television shows such as "America's Funniest Home Videos," or "Planet's Funniest Animals," which airs on the cable network, Animal Planet. It's not only fun to see your *masterpiece* on TV, but some of these shows offer generous prizes for outstanding videos.

Also, when you do gather together all the video you shot at the student recitals we mentioned above, someone will have to look at them. They make for much pleasanter viewing if you can edit them into a cohesive, entertaining package with *blends, wipes, fade ins, fade outs,* and maybe a few witty title cards to add some laughs.

Docent:

This activity involves volunteering (maybe a few of them pay) to work at a nearby place of interest. Docents conduct tours of the facility or serve as a guide who directs people around the tour site. You'd be required to research the place so that you could offer helpful guidance to the tourists and answer most of their questions.

Dog Training:

If you have confidence with animals and they seem to have trust in you, this could be a worthwhile endeavor for you. Dog training can be a one-on-one activity—you and one dog—or you could be an instructor for group classes. Perhaps you'd be interested in learning this skill just so you can teach your own pet not to chew your slippers. In any form, it will require some ingenuity. It's not easy to outsmart a canine.

Doll Making:

If dolls fascinated you when you were young, they could intrigue you even more now that you've reached the over-forty-nine plateau. There are many levels to this craft. Some people can make beautiful playthings out of a few pieces of Styrofoam and a hank of wool. Maybe rag dolls would be of interest to you—like Raggedy Ann and Andy. Or, you may aspire to the higher level of dollmaking, creating beautiful sewn costumes and intricately carved faces.

Dress Making:

This activity includes a degree of designing and a lot of skillful needlework. You can design and make your own clothes, clothes for others, doll clothes, and even make costumes for plays.

Faux Painting:

"Faux" is a French word for "false" or "fake." In this activity you paint things to look like something they're not. If you have pillars in your home, you may paint them to appear to be marble. You may paint a wall to look like brickwork. There are all sorts of deceptive, yet practical uses you can make of this skill. It's fun, it's creative, and it's quite useful.

Filmmaking:

Steven Spielberg began his impressive career as a youngster with a store-bought home movie camera. You can do the same thing. You may not go on to the fame and fortune of Spielberg, but you can produce some entertaining short pieces or you can produce some enlightening documentaries.

Flower Arranging:

This artistic activity involves creating appealing still lifes using real plants and flowers. With this activity you assemble cut flowers into beautiful bouquets, sprays, and centerpieces.

Flower Making:

With this activity you can not only arrange gorgeous bouquets, but also make the flowers that you arrange. You can replicate roses, carnations—almost any flower you want—with materials as simple as colored paper or silk. In fact, you can create varieties of plants that don't even exist. You wrap, twist, and mold the paper or silk to whatever form you desire. If it looks like a flower and is beautiful, who cares if no botanist can categorize it? That's the luxury and the license of creativity.

Gardening:

This activity doesn't need much explanation. All it needs is some soil, some fertilizer, and a good strong back. It's not only a creative activity, but good exercise, too. It is a pastime that will get your hands dirty, but it's a good, clean kind of dirt.

Genealogy:

Find some ancestors who were famous. Maybe find a few who were infamous, villainous, raunchy, or whatever. When you start your search you never know quite what you'll find in your line of relatives. It takes a bit of detective work to trace your lineage as far back as you can.

Handicapping Sports Events:

Anybody can be a good Monday morning quarterback. It's easy to look back and pontificate on what the athletes or coaches should have done or could have done. However, it takes real know-how to predict what is going to happen in any given sporting event.

This activity requires a solid knowledge of sports, investigative research, some common sense, and a dash of creativity. Match your knowledge of sports against the *experts* who predict the outcome of the games or the races in the newspaper. See if you can't produce better results than they do.

Handwriting Analysis:

This is an interesting field and there are countless books on the subject, schools that teach handwriting analysis, and associations devoted to the field. It can be useful in many ways. Businesses use it to develop personality profiles for prospective employees, counselors use it to focus their advice on a client's particular personality concerns, and some people use it to determine potential compatibility.

Of course, it makes a great diversion at social gatherings if you're tactful enough not to lose some friends.

There is a difference between a handwriting expert and a handwriting analyst. The expert uses his knowledge for forensic purposes, to determine if certain signatures and letters are authentic or forged. The analyst focuses more on personality peculiarities for businesses, counseling, and vocational guidance.

Home Brewing (Beer and Wine):

It's legal.

Interior Decorating:

This is a challenging field that involves a good artistic sense, a feel for blending colors, an eye for the efficient and pleasing use of space, and also knowledge of what to buy, where to buy it, and how to get a good price.

Investing:

Will Rogers summed this talent up with his one-liner, "If your stock goes up in value, sell. If it doesn't go up in value, don't buy it in the first place." This activity satisfies both your business knowledge and your gambling inclinations.

You don't need tons of money to invest like a power broker, either. This is an activity that you can get caught up in even if you're playing with make-believe money. The problem with this, though, is that if you do make a big killing in the market, you will kick yourself for not having the real cash invested.

Jewelry Making:

This seems to be a quite popular hobby and potential business. If you have a good sense of design, some artistic skills, and a love of jewelry, this might interest you.

There are many facets to it—making chandelier earrings, fabricating metal jewelry, bead stringing, macramé jewelry, metal clay jewelry, and many others.

There are books on the subject, Internet lessons are available, and some adult education classes may be offered locally.

Knitting:

My mother and sister knitted endlessly. Mom made me all sorts of gorgeous sweaters and scarves. Mom and Sis could do wonders with wool, and so can you.

My only connection with this skill (and it's a fond memory) is that I would hold the hank of wool that Mom and my sister brought home from the store so they could roll it into a ball. I would stretch my hands apart and then move them from side to side as they unraveled the hank of yarn and wound it into a ball. I was very good at that, but I never made any sweaters.

Learn to Play a Musical Instrument:

If you have music in your soul, it's good to let it out occasionally. You can only do this if you can play an instrument—guitar, piano, even drums if your family and neighbors can stand it.

To make this pursuit worthwhile, you don't have to become a maestro. All you have to do is learn enough to be able to pick out a few tunes by ear or learn to read music. Playing for you own pleasure is just as rewarding as playing in Carnegie Hall.

Learn a New Sport:

What's so creative about this? Anyone can pick up a set of golf clubs, rent some shoes at the bowling alley, or grab a racket and a can of tennis balls, and play. That's true, but the creative angle we're talking about here is discovering a way to learn a particular sport well and design a practice schedule that will help you improve.

In other words, with this activity, you commit to becoming a fairly competent player. You read about the techniques of the sport, you analyze your own game, and you set goals for your improvement.

All of this should keep you occupied for some time.

Learn a New Language:

I remember a joke Bob Hope once used when a guest spoke to him in a foreign language. Hope responded with, "I can speak French. Hasta la vista." The guest corrected him. "That's Spanish." Hope, surprised, said, "That's Spanish?" The guest said it was. Bob Hope then replied, "Oh, then I speak three languages."

Of course, there's more to knowing a language than learning a few phrases. There's vocabulary, grammar, idioms, and lot's more. It requires dedication, perseverance, and study.

The creative aspect of this is in designing a study schedule that will help you learn all you need to know, n'est-ce pas?

Learn to Use Computers:

A few of us in the over-fifty category may be behind the times when it comes to using this new magnificent tool—the home computer. I remember sitting at my monitor with my ten-year-old granddaughter. We had called up a photograph that we wanted to print, but I explained to her that I had no way of transferring that image from the screen to my printer. Without saying a word, she grabbed the mouse, moved it somewhere, clicked something, and several icons appeared in the upper left hand corner of the photograph. She clicked the "printer" icon and my computer spit out a full-color printout of the image.

Who knew?

Computers can do magic, but often only if the operator is the magician. The machines can only do what they're told. The field is confusing, but intriguing and conquerable.

Magic:

The field of real magic is almost as diverse as the above-mentioned computer magic. There is close-up magic where the performer can do all of his tricks while surrounded by onlookers. There is stage illusion in which the magician can make cars, elephants, or whatever disappear and reappear. There is sleight of hand which requires skill, dexterity, and practice. There is mechanical magic where the trick itself does all the work; all you supply is the "patter" to accompany and explain it. There are card tricks, rope tricks, and coin tricks. The list goes on and on.

There are standard tricks like the Linking Rings, the Balls and Cups, the Torn and Restored Newspaper, and catalogues full of other amazing and entertaining illusions. Countless books are available on all forms and styles of magic and supply houses sell the various tricks, along with the instructions on how to perform them.

The real creativity of magic—in any of its many forms—is the presentation. That's where most of your creativity will come in.

Making Stained Glass Windows:

Working in stained glass requires the creativity of an artist in designing the decorative pieces, whether they're actual windows or simply an artistic panel of colored glass. It also requires the mechanical skills required to assemble the many pieces of the design into one work of art.

A quick check of the Internet showed that there are many instructional videos and books on this art form. One of these—*Basic Stained Glass Making: All the Skill and Tools You'll Need to Get Started* by Eric Ebeling, Michael Johnson, and Alay Wycheck—seemed to offer everything that a beginning stained glass artist might need. It offered safety tips, tools that are needed, some design ideas, and so on.

The back cover of the book pictured a stained glass lampshade, several decorative wall hangings, a mirror decorated with a stained glass rose, and a three-dimensional hanging snowflake. So there are plenty of practical uses for this creative endeavor.

Metallic Leafing:

Art stores and catalogues offer several forms of this craft—gold, silver, imitation gold and silver, copper, and several other interesting variations. The leaf is just that—an ultra thin layer of metal that you attach to whatever it is you're trying to decorate. You can revitalize old lamps with this craft. You can apply an attractive finish to a piece of sculpture. You can rejuvenate old pieces of furniture.

Miniatures and Dollhouses:

Just as maintaining, furnishing, and decorating a real house is a never-ending adventure, so is maintaining, furnishing, and decorating a dollhouse. Whether you buy a small-sized house or build your own, it will need painting, wall papering, floor coverings—all part of this creative endeavor.

You can shop for interesting furniture for your dollhouse or you can buy furniture kits to build the various pieces. You can also design and make furniture on your own.

You can redecorate, renovate, and refurnish your tiny home.

This is a creative activity that can keep you interested and entertained for years.

Model Railroading:

There was a joke years ago about two inebriated buddies walking along the streets of New York. As they strolled, one happened to walk down the steps of a subway entrance. The other continued on. Later, they reunited when the one came back up the steps from the subway. One gentleman turned to the other and said, "Where'd you go?" The other said, "I don't know. I was walking along and suddenly I was in someone's basement. I tell you this…the guy has a fabulous set of trains."

When I was a kid at boarding school, every year I'd be assigned to help out with "the platform." That's what we called the toy villages that were set up with a set of trains running around them. Our platform at school was unique, though, because one of the teachers was a model railroad enthusiast. He built all his own trains and trolley cars. The village we set up each Christmas was about 15 x 30 inches in size. All buildings in the village were handmade, as were all of the railroad trains, elevated cars, and street cars that ran through it.

We workers assembled the set each holiday season, but it was really one man's work of art. So, model railroading can be as intricate and creative as you want it to be.

Model Building:

This can include models of all sorts—airplanes, ships, cars, or covered wagons. Regardless what may interest you, you can probably find a model kit available. The kits can range in complexity, too. Some simply involve snap-together-and-glue procedures. Others can include working with wood, trimming pieces to size, and, with old time ships, you may even have to trim the sails and run the rigging from mast to mast.

You might even choose to design and build your own models from scratch.

Mosaics:

This is an art form in which you assemble small pieces of tile, glass, or stones of varying colors to form a picture or design. This activity requires an artist's eye, along with a dexterity that enables you to cut the pieces and affix them to the artwork.

The results can be astonishing.

Movie or TV Reviewing:

Do you enjoy analyzing shows? Do you have a keen eye for the director's expertise? Do you know and appreciate good acting? Can you determine whether a particular film or TV show is well-written or not? Then maybe you can pass your learned opinion on to others in the form of reviews. You could write them for your local paper or your office newsletter, or just to pass them along to friends.

Organize a Charity Event:

At most conventions, seminars, and workshops there are countless people making speeches, glad-handing one another, and accepting accolades and awards. Then there is one person behind the scenes who really knows what's going on and keeps it going on—and on schedule, too. That's the organizer—the brains behind the operation.

This is a worthy project for worthy causes that might interest you.

Organize a Profit-Making Event:

Heck, as long as you're at it, you might as well make a buck.

Oriental Brush Calligraphy and Painting:

With just a few twists of the brush, you can form interesting designs and artwork. It's an ancient, challenging, and intriguing skill. Art suppliers can furnish the implements you'll need and also offer several books that teach the technique.

Paint with Oils, Acrylics, or Watercolors:

Each of these different mediums has its own advantages and tribulations. The resulting product of each has its own rewards, too. You may have to experiment to see which one you can work best in, but they're all fun and waiting for your own touch of creativity.

Pantomimist:

Once you say "pantomimist," there's nothing more to say. It's an art form where you convey your meaning through actions and gestures only. Marcel Marceau was a famous "mime," and comedian Red Skelton used pantomime in many of his comedy routines. Most circus clowns depend on it for their shenanigans, too.

It requires some skill to perform and considerable ingenuity to create.

Party Planning:

This is an activity that is more complicated than it might appear. Putting together a well-organized party involves many different facets. As the organizer you may have to come up with the theme, decide on decorations, create appealing center pieces, finalize the best date and time, design invitations, arrange the seating (so that you don't have Uncle Martin sitting anywhere near Aunt Sarah, since they haven't spoken to each other in years), book the band and entertainment, and plan the program of events.

It's a daunting task, but it might be just what you're looking for.

Pencil or Charcoal Drawing:

You know how some movies seem to be more dramatic and effective in black-and-white? The same can apply to certain works of art. A nice pencil or charcoal sketch often has more impact than a painting. This creative activity is relatively inexpensive, too. All you really need is a piece of paper, a sharp pencil or stick of charcoal, and perhaps a good eraser, too.

Photography:

Everyone is familiar with this art form. Digital cameras and computer software programs have made this activity that much more astounding. Also, with digital cameras you can produce your pictures instantly and much more inexpensively.

Picture Framing and Matting:

A nice photo or work of art always looks more appealing when it's matted and framed properly. With a relatively inexpensive mat cutter, you can enhance any picture with a creative border. The nice part of cutting your own mats is that you can add creativity and flair. I saw a drawing someone once did of the great comedian George Burns. When he cut his own mat, the artist snipped out a little edge so that George's ubiquitous cigar overlapped the border.

Playing Poker:

Television has made this a popular pastime. The game requires considerable skill, but creativity is important, too—knowing how much to bet, when to bet, and how to make your opponents think you know what you're doing.

Pottery:

This is the art of making a vessel from clay. The piece must first be designed, then *thrown* on a pottery wheel. The glazing, firing, and final decorative painting are all part of this creative project.

Public Relations or Publicity Campaign:

A story told about Bob Hope's early career days illustrates how important publicity can be. Hope, a fledgling radio personality at the time, was making several personal appearances at theaters around the country. One weekend the gentleman who handled his publicity visited him backstage after the show. Hope said kiddingly, "What are you doing here? Why aren't you making me famous?" The PR guy said, "Bob, it's Sunday. All the offices are closed." Hope said, "Why can't you go door-to-door?"

This activity can be a challenging creative project. You must write interesting, eye-catching press releases, design ads, arrange interviews, and do whatever you can to get this particular event before the public.

Many service clubs, organizations, churches, and associations you belong to have fundraising events each year. Handling the publicity and advertising for these affairs can be not only time-consuming, but creatively fascinating.

Puppeteering:

There are many variations of this activity—string puppets, handheld puppets, and several others. The fun can come from designing and making your own figures and also in manipulating them. You might also get involved in writing the scripts for your "actors" to perform.

Quilting:

This is an activity that requires a steady hand and an artist's sense of design. It's also a social function because many of the quilts are designed, stitched, and assembled by a group of people. The end product is something that can be cherished as a family heirloom for many years.

Refurbishing Junk (toy trucks, for example):

Once, while visiting friends in Arizona, a neighbor invited us to tour his workshop. It was actually his garage. In there he had shelves and shelves of beautiful metal toy trucks. They were shiny and colorful. I thought he was a collector. Then he showed me his current project. It was a beat-up, rusted old tractor that looked more dangerous than appealing.

That, however, was his hobby—finding worthless toy vehicles and fixing them up. He would add wheels, levers, hinges—whatever the toy needed to become functional once again. Then he would paint and polish them to make them look brand new.

The transition from junk to masterpiece was incredible.

You could repair and restore old watches or clocks. You could refurbish some tired, worn-out appliances. This activity can include practically anything that once looked beautiful and worked, but now doesn't. But it will when you get done with it.

Scrapbooking:

This pursuit has gained much prominence in recent years. Craft stores offer various useful products to help add some flair to your pages. Of course, the computer and printer also add versatility to your layouts.

The finished scrapbooks make great gifts and terrific mementos of whatever event you're capturing within the front and back covers.

Sculpture:

This venture covers many variations—clay, marble, wood, and any other media that can be shaped, carved, or molded into portraits, figures, or abstract designs. It's a challenging endeavor, because while painting and sketching involve only two dimensions, sculpting requires the use of a third dimension. However, this aspect makes the finished product all the more satisfying.

Sewing:

This activity is self-explanatory. It involves not only being handy with a needle and thread but also having a sense of design. If you know your way around a sewing machine and can thread a needle without going cross-eyed, you might also introduce some creativity to this activity. My mom used to take great joy and pride in creating fashionable, glamorous, glitzy clothes for her grandchildren's Barbie dolls.

Shopper:

What can be more fun than going shopping? Especially with someone else's money. Many busy executives, organizations, social clubs, and others need not only advice on what to buy for special occasions, but also someone to go out into the marketplace and find those special gifts…and at a bargain price.

Singing:

Whenever my wife and I are driving and I hear a Frank Sinatra, Bobby Darin, or Dean Martin song on the radio, I say, "That's what I should have been—a saloon singer." My wife invariably responds, "It's not too late."

And she's right. I could buy myself a tux, get booked in some club or another, and sing to the people as they get up and leave.

However, there are other singing possibilities besides being the lone crooner behind the microphone. There are church choirs, perhaps choral groups where you work, or you could do background vocalizing for a local band.

Also, there's a national organization of dedicated and devoted singers called SPEBSQSA (pronounced SPEBSQSA). Those initials stand for the "Society for the Preservation and Encouragement of Barbershop Quartet Singing in America." This is a fine association that has chapters all over the nation. Most of them put on annual shows, sponsor contests, and hand out awards. Mostly, though, they provide an outlet for folks who just love to harmonize.

Soap Making:

I suppose in the old days, this was more a necessity than a pastime. Today, however, it's become more of an art form. The soaps can be made into fancy statuettes that have the ability to work up a lather. They can be artfully decorated and colored, and of course, scented. In fact, the soaps can be anything your creativity can devise.

Sports Coaching:

Someone once joked that the only people who really know how to run our government are all driving cabs or tending bar. The same is true of sports. The only people who know how to coach their local professional squad to a championship are the guys who sit in front of a television and berate the guys who are being paid to coach.

Now is a fine time to exercise some of that expertise you have. Maybe you won't land a high-paying professional assignment at first, but you can surely start with the youngsters who are eager to play tee ball.

These youngsters need to know the basics and you can surely teach those. At the same time, you'll enjoy the experience of being involved in sports and getting to know and earn the respect of a lot of enthusiastic kids.

Stamp Collecting:

There are many interesting facets to stamp collecting. Some philatelists (that's the fancy word for stamp collectors) endeavor to acquire rare and expensive stamps. Others work to build collections of more commonplace stamps in various categories. For instance, some may collect stamps from certain countries. There are those who are interested in stamps featuring animals in general or a specific animal, like butteflies. Some people enjoy collecting stamps with depictions of plants and flowers. Political figures, show business personalities, sports celebrities, or historic events are other types of stamps people may collect.

A creative part of stamp collecting, too, is the display of your stamps. Many stamp shows have judging and prizes for the exhibition of stamps in various categories.

Stand-up Comedy:

The late Steve Allen commented on the popularity of stand-up comedy—"Every kid used to have a guitar. Now every kid has six minutes that he can do at the local comedy club." Stand-up comedy is a challenging endeavor. When comedy is done well, it seems easy. Well-conceived and performed stand-up almost sounds like the comic is thinking the jokes up *on the spot.* He or she is not. It takes imagination to create or research the jokes, and skill in presenting them believably. But the sound of the audience's laughter makes it all worthwhile.

Once Bob Hope went on a vacation to a remote fishing spot. He was scheduled to be away for two weeks. He called me for new material after about two days. I said, "I thought you were fishing in Alaska." He said, "I was. I found out that fish don't applaud." That's how strong the lure of an appreciative audience can be.

Of course, comedy is not limited only to the microphone at the comedy club. You can present small monologues at your service club meetings, at parties with your fellow employees, at functions with the folks you bowl with or play golf, tennis, or bridge with.

Storytelling:

Storytelling is just what it says—telling interesting and unusual stories with enthusiasm and flair. These can be stories told at historic places about that particular location. You might specialize in tales about your particular area. It's possible that service clubs in certain regions may be interested in some unique myths, legends, or fables about their specific locale. If you can research anecdotes and relate them with gusto, you can surely find an outlet.

Often bookstores and libraries seek out people to tell children's stories or read children's books a few times a week.

If you like to add drama to a narrative, this could be your field.

Tap Dancing:

This is not only a fun outlet for all that rhythm you've got built up inside your soul, but it's also fantastic exercise. It's probably more of a cardiovascular workout than most exercise programs.

Teaching:

This activity can be at any level—K through 12, adult education classes, teaching special skills like painting or jewelry making, or passing on some of your business experience to other workers in your field.

It's a rewarding project because the information you pass on can go on forever. Someone learns what you teach and presumably passes it on to someone else, and so on and on.

Tutoring:

Tutoring is similar to teaching and it yields the same satisfaction. This may be a bit more specialized, though, where you work one-on-one with someone who needs a little more help in a particular subject that is difficult for him or her.

Voice-over:

"Voice-over" refers to reading lines or dialogue for television, even though you're not seen on the screen. It can be the dialogue that you hear in commercials or documentaries or it can be providing the line readings for cartoon characters.

Some celebrities prefer voice-overs to actually appearing in commercials. Generally, when you do a commercial, your contract will prevent you from appearing on-screen promoting rival products. With voice-overs, though, you're usually free to do as many as you like and even for competing companies.

This activity requires a pleasant voice, the ability to read copy quickly, adjust your delivery to the time constraints of TV, and some training. Of course, the marketing of your talents is another creative aspect of this pursuit.

Web Page Design:

Almost everything and everyone today has a web page. Even folks who don't know anything at all about the Internet have a website. There's a demand for people who know something about both computers and design to create the web pages that people want to promote themselves and their businesses.

Wedding Consultant (and/or Planner):

Marriage used to be between a bride and a groom. Nowadays it's between the bride, the groom, and the wedding consultant. If your wedding is to be in a church, a chapel, or a temple, most likely a wedding consultant will be *de rigueur.* A wedding consultant assists with the decorations, the wedding rehearsal, the selection of music, organizing the traffic of guests as they arrive, and, of course, telling the bride and groom where to go, what to do, and any other details required.

Wood Carving:

This activity involves sculpting with wood. All you really need to get started is a whittling or carving knife (although, of course, there are more complicated tools that you may want to or need to add as you progress), some ideas, a fairly steady hand, and a chunk of wood.

There are many clubs devoted to wood carving around the country. A quick trip to the Internet can furnish contacts for these. There are also books on the craft and magazines devoted exclusively to it.

As you read through the books, the magazines, or the Internet sites, you'll discover classes in wood carving for all levels, from beginner to advanced.

Write a "How-To" Book:

Regardless of what you know, there is always someone out there who doesn't know as much as you do about a particular topic, but would like to know more. You can pass on whatever you know to whoever wants to know it. The perfect vehicle for accomplishing this is the "how-to" book. Of course, they're not always called "how-to" books. They have all sorts of clever, appealing titles. There's *Chess for Dummies, The Complete Idiot's Guide to Music Theory, The Plane Truth for Golfers*, and there's even one called *Unleashing Your Creativity Over 50!* These are all fancy names for "how-to" books.

There are even "how-to" books that will teach you how to write "how-to" books.

I always wanted to write a book called *Ventriloquism for Dummies*.

Write a Book of Poetry:

A gentleman who wrote humor for some of the legends of comedy and produced and wrote many of the most popular and well-received shows on television used to begin each working day by writing a limerick. He called this his "heart starter." It was like his warm-up exercise. When he could turn out an amusing, well-written, five-line rhyming poem, he felt he was ready to face the serious business of churning out television comedy.

When he retired from TV, he wrote a book of serious poetry—with a dash of humor to make it more readable. He published this collection at his own expense and distributed the books only to family and friends.

It was a cathartic exercise for him and the thoughts he expressed in his eloquent style are always there for those friends and relatives to enjoy.

Writing poetry is not only an imaginative way of getting your thoughts about everything onto paper, but it can also create a legacy that lasts a long time.

Write a Children's Book:

One caution here at the outset—writing a book for children is not *easier* than writing a book for adults. In many ways it's more difficult. You have to work with ideas that youngsters can handle. You must explain your thoughts using a vocabulary that children can comprehend. You should be cautious of the ideas that you promote.

So this is not a project you begin because it seems *simpler* than other writing endeavors.

However, it is a challenging and rewarding endeavor. If you have stories you want to tell to youngsters and ideas that you want to convey, this is a fun way to do it.

Write a Cookbook:

Anyone who cooks enjoys the adventure of trying a new recipe. Anyone who has created an exciting recipe is eager to pass it on to others.

Half of the imagination in assembling a cookbook is conceiving the theme that holds it all together. There are cookbooks featuring recipes that the cooks used when they manned the chuck wagon during cattle drives. There are cookbooks featuring favorite recipes from restaurants all over the world. There are those listing dishes that various celebrities enjoyed.

My daughter "published" a family cookbook as Christmas presents for her parents and brothers and sisters. She presented the recipes for the family members' favorite meals and the dishes they most liked to cook. Of course, each page also had a bit of humorous narrative about some event—happy or otherwise—that happened in connection with each recipe. She also featured some hilarious, unflattering photographs.

Assembling a cookbook is a worthwhile project whether you have it published or merely assemble it yourself.

Write a Newspaper Column:

Everyone has something worthwhile—or at least something they consider worthwhile—to contribute to the community. Put your thoughts on paper, in 850 or so words, and contribute it to your local newspaper or to national syndicates.

What do you write about? Anything that interests you. If you enjoy sports, write about the high school games in your area. Do you enjoy going to the movies? Publish a weekly review of the latest films in your area weekly. Maybe you can offer household hints to your readers. How about human interest stories? If you're courageous enough, you might even comment on local government and politics.

Write a Novel:

What a great creative undertaking—to write the next Great American Novel. Develop a premise, devise plot points, create characters (good and evil), and tell a story that is a real "page-turner."

Many authors will tell you that once you create your characters and the story you're going to tell, you almost sit back and let the characters narrate that tale for you. You watch them in your head and write down what they say and do.

Some folks will warn you that it's difficult to interest publishers in a first novel written by an unproven writer. So what? The fun, remember, is in the doing.

Write Short Stories:

Maybe doing a novel of 80,000 to 120,000 words is too daunting a task. Fine, you can still tell stories. You can tell an interesting tale in 2,000 words or less. And you can produce a lot more of them.

Write Comedy:

Do you enjoy Leno's one-liners? Letterman's classic quips? Why not try to write a few of your own? It's not that difficult. To try, all you need is a sheet of paper, a pen, and an active, off-beat imagination.

It's nice to send some to celebrities and hear your one-liners on TV, or to send them to columnists and read your witty remarks in the paper. However, it's also a fun and useful project even if you never even try to sell a joke.

People love to laugh. You can assemble collections of pictures and captions to give to friends on special occasions—birthdays, anniversaries, graduations, and such. You can also write your own greeting cards to accompany gifts—cards with funny comments that are unique to the people receiving them.

You might even work up the courage to volunteer to emcee the next club meeting or party using your own self-generated monologue.

(This is a bold-faced, self-serving promotional note, but an excellent primer for gag writing is my own book, *The New Comedy Writing Step by Step*, published by Quill Driver Books.)

Write Greeting Card Verses and Jokes:

Greeting cards are a big business. They're no longer reserved for Christmas, birthdays, and the like. Nowadays there are cards for every occasion and even some for no occasion at all.

You might combine this with the previous suggestion and write humorous cards, which are tremendously popular. Or, you could write sentimental thoughts that any friend would be happy to receive.

Write Plays:

There's a story told about Neil "Doc" Simon, the great Broadway playwright. Doc was visiting his old neighborhood in New York and decided to stop in at the candy store where he and his buddies used to hang out as youngsters. The proprietor was still "on duty" in the store and Simon introduced himself. The candy store owner said, "Little Neil Simon. It's great to see you. What are you doing nowadays?" Simon said, "Oh, I write plays for Broadway." The owner said, "Really. How much do you make doing that?" Simon said, "Oh, about $50,000 a week." The proprietor said, "No kidding! I should have gone into that business."

Well, now *you* can go into that business. If you have an idea you want to convey, a story you want to tell, maybe a three-act play could be your calling.

Remember, too, that it doesn't necessarily have to be for Broadway. It can be for your church group. It can be a play for your son's or daughter's fifth-grade class. It can be a short skit that you perform before your service club.

* * *

So there—there are 101 creative activities which might interest you. Come to think of it, another worthwhile creative project might be to go back and count these suggestions to make sure that there really are 101 of them. Have fun.

Chapter 12

Beginning Your Creativity Activity

The first step of any journey begins with…well…it begins with the first step. That first step in any venture is to learn something about that particular activity.

There are two parts to this knowledge you're about to acquire. The first part is intellectual information. It's data that you gather and store in your mind—or in a notebook that you keep.

Just to illustrate, let's suppose that you're a raw beginner who wants to learn to play golf—to hit a golf ball correctly. You learn that to hit a golf ball, you'll first need a golf ball. Golf balls, for all practical purposes, come in only one size and shape. The ball is round and has a diameter of 1.68 inches (there are exceptions to that diameter, but that's not relevant here). However, there are different specifications for golf balls that may be relevant. Different golf balls can have a different number of dimples. They can have different cores—wound, solid, or multi-layer. There are different types of covers, and varying compression ratings. One compression may be perfect for professional players with a fast swing velocity, but not ideal for higher-handicap players. Being aware of all these variations can be helpful in determining which ball is optimum for you, a beginner.

You'll learn also that to hit a golf ball, you'll need a golf club. The "sticks" can be even more complex than the ball. There are steel shafts and graphite shafts. These shafts can have different flex ratings—light, regular, or stiff. The kick point of these shafts can be low, mid, or high. The club head can be offset on the shaft, or traditional. Even the grips can be made of different materials, have varying textures, and come in different sizes. How do all these variables relate to your swing as a beginner? Being aware of the different alternatives may help you decide which clubs are best suited to the beginning golfer and which ones are best designed for your body size and type.

Next, you should know, intellectually, how to correctly swing a golf club.

And there's so much more.

This is the part of beginning a new project that we'll call "Research." We'll discuss the reasons for and the "how-to" of research in the following chapter.

* * *

Even with the appropriate ball, the best designed set of clubs, and a knowledge of the mechanical aspects of the golf swing, the beginner probably still can't hit the ball accurately and well. This requires a practical, hands-on knowledge of striking the ball.

A first time golfer can tee up a $12 golf ball that most of the professionals prefer, stand over it with a marvelously engineered and manufactured golf club, swing at it with all of the stored up knowledge about the perfect golf swing that he or she has acquired, and dribble the ball about 20 yards down the fairway, rather than the 310 yards that Tiger Woods might smack it.

Yes, the beginner now has to hit golf ball after golf ball after golf ball. The beginner must gain some experience and learn from personal experimentation and observation, get qualified feedback from a qualified instructor, and learn how to hit the ball correctly and consistently.

This is the part of beginning a new project that we'll call "Learning." We'll discuss the reason and the "how-to" for this aspect in Chapter 14.

Remember, we've chosen beginning golf as an illustration only. The same principles, though, apply to almost any creative project you want to initiate.

Now let's move on to "Research."

Chapter 13

Research

A few bigwigs were touring a post office and they watched as the employees were busy sorting mail. Each postal worker in his or her particular style would glance at the address and then place that envelope into one of many slots set to receive it. They worked with varying levels of skill and efficiency. Then the executives came to one particular employee who was flying through his batch of mail. He'd go through the letters fast and flip them into the various cubicles like he was a machine. The letters zipped in and out of his hands in a fraction of a second.

One of the executives approached this worker and complimented him on his speed and prowess. He said, "You're the fastest letter sorter I've ever seen in my many years in the postal service." The man thanked him humbly. "Well, I appreciate that, sir, and I'll tell you this, I'll go even faster once I learn how to read."

We have to know what we're doing if we're going to do it well. That's one of the reasons why it's important to begin a new creative activity with some research. Here are a few others:

1. To Gain a General Knowledge of the Field:

Many of the creative activities you might be interested in are commonplace. You probably have a *general* awareness of what they are and what they entail. You know what stamp collecting is. You know what oil painting is. However, there may be a few that are less obvious. Metallic leafing may be a mystery to some. A few readers, like me, might have to look up "decoupage" in the dictionary.

Some research into all fields is beneficial, though, because even if you do know a little bit about something, your research may uncover important facets of that field that you are not aware of.

2. To Gain Specialized Knowledge of the Field:

Earlier, I mentioned that my five-year-old grandson took a series of tennis lessons for beginning youngsters. When the club offered a series of follow-up lessons, I asked if he would be interested in those. He said, "No. I know all there is to know about tennis now."

Many of us may feel the same way about certain activities and then are astounded to discover after some research that the more we think we know, the less we really know. Perhaps it would be more accurate to say that the more we learn, the more we learn that we have much more to learn. In a previous chapter, we learned the intricacies of something so apparently simple as a golf club. There are different shafts, flex ratings, kick points, and so on.

It's always amazing to me when I watch shows on television about woodworking that there seems to be an "attachment" for every conceivable occasion. The host will say something like, "Now I have to make an offset cut with an interlocking flanged fitting at a 45-degree angle." Sounds impossible, doesn't it? The host then says, "So, I'll simply add my 'offset cut with interlocking flanged fitting attachment' and set it at a 45-degree angle." Who knew such a thing ever existed? (And it may not exist because I made up all those terms and have no idea what they mean, but you get my point.)

When I took my first course in sculpting, I pushed and molded the clay and completed a fairly representative piece that I was proud of. Like my grandson, *I knew all there was to know about sculpting.* Later, I met with some professional sculptors and one asked, "Do you use water-based or oil-based clay?" I had no idea. I used what the teacher gave me. I didn't even know there were two kinds of sculpting clay. Nor did I have any idea what the advantages and disadvantages of each were. Another asked, "Are you going to have it cast using the 'lost wax' method or 'cold casting'?" Again, I had no idea because I had never heard of either method and didn't know which was preferred for my particular piece.

Research not only helps you learn much about a specific activity, but it also teaches you *what you don't know*. It can aid in learning the importance of and usefulness of searching out what you don't yet know, and it can offer suggestions on where and how to find the answers to any questions prompted by this new information.

Any activity you select will have hidden complexities that will keep you learning more and more regardless of how long you practice. Someone once suggested that a specialist is *someone who knows more and more about less and less and that the perfect specialist is someone who knows all there is to know about absolutely nothing*. It's almost true. With an interesting creative pursuit, you can continue to learn endlessly.

Your initial research needn't provide all the knowledge. But it can make you aware of many of the questions. Then you can seek out the answers to those questions that will benefit your work.

3. Research Helps You Know what Equipment or Tools You'll Need:

Each activity has its own array of tools. An artist requires brushes and paints; a furniture maker needs power tools and that limitless supply of 'attachments' mentioned earlier. A photographer needs a camera and film (although nowadays *digital* photography is the rage); a jewelry maker needs a pair of long-nosed pliers.

Research will tell you what equipment is essential—what you'll absolutely need to *get started*. It will offer comparative costs of these tools and suggest vendors or stores where you can obtain this equipment.

As item 2 suggested, you may learn considerably more about your craft as you gain more experience in it. So you may want to begin your activity with minimal equipment. Going back to the golf clubs example, it may not be advantageous to buy the most expensive and best-engineered equipment simply because it's available. As you continue to play, learn, and improve, you may discover exactly which shafts, flexibility, and kick points are best suited to your playing style. The same is most likely true for whichever activity you engage in.

Nevertheless, research will tell you what equipment is available. As I mentioned earlier, I'm always amazed at the number of *attachments* that simplify complicated woodworking tasks. However, they only simplify the tasks if the carpenter is aware of them and uses them.

In making authentic wooden models of ships, often the wooden components are nailed together. Considering the miniaturization of the vessels themselves, you can imagine how miniscule the nails are. Imagine trying to hold one in place with your fingers as you try to hammer it into the wood. Shipbuilding catalogues, though, offer a tool that allows you to easily "punch" the nail into the timber. It's a very useful tool, but only if you know it exists.

Earlier we wondered if Michelangelo actually took a hammer and chisel to the marble. If he did, do power tools now exist that help artists perform the same task more easily, more quickly, and more delicately? Research should answer this question.

Through your research, too, you will become aware of the various specifications of the equipment. Let's go back to our golf club example. Not every golfer is aware of the modifications available or what purpose each modification serves. For example, what does a low kick point accomplish for your swing? Will a flexible shaft or a stiff shaft be more likely to improve your game?

If you're involved in scrapbooking, what kinds of glue are available? Will they discolor over time? Which offer the best value— effectiveness versus cost? Which adhesives are the easiest to use? I remember trying to build a model airplane and I would have more tiny parts stuck to my fingers than to each other. Naturally, I blamed this on the quality of the airplane cement rather than on my dexterity.

For painters, which type of paint produces the easiest application and color consistency? For a digital photographer, how many pixels are required to yield the quality of picture required?

In whatever activity you select, it's important to know what type of equipment is available and exactly which type you'll require for your purposes.

The following personal example shows how important the right equipment and the right specifications can be. As a youngster, I began doing some oil painting under the tutelage of a very accomplished artist. For my birthday one year, my parents bought me a set of good quality paint brushes. I was thrilled. I loved the feel of them in my hands. Unfortunately, when I tried to paint with them, they were totally useless. The bristles weren't strong enough to spread the paint on the canvas.

They were short handled brushes. We later learned that those were designed for watercolor painting. Oil painting required longer-handled brushes with much stiffer bristles.

The specifications of the equipment are important and your research tells you what is right for your tasks.

Research can also determine, or at least advise about, the quality of the equipment. The brushes my folks bought for me in the above illustration were top-quality artist brushes. They were not inexpensive. They simply were not designed for the work that I was doing. However, there is good quality equipment and bad quality equipment. There's also equipment that is good enough for the task at a reasonable price. Which you select is your choice, but your research lets you know which is which.

A Rolls-Royce is a wonderful car, but perhaps a tad too expensive for most of us. Yet we also don't want a used "junker" that may fall apart with the first bump it hits in the road. We must weigh quality against cost, but to do that we must become aware of the quality. That's where the research is necessary.

Doing your research gives you an idea of the cost of the equipment. We all want a good bargain for our money, so your investigation can help you shop around for competitive prices on whatever supplies you'll need. Learning about the cost of materials for your potential creative project can also be a determining factor in whether you pursue that activity or not. Is it too expensive for your budget? You can't know the answer to that until you know approximately how much it's going to cost.

Just for the purpose of comparison, let's suppose you're a raw beginner with absolutely no equipment. To begin pencil sketching, you'll require a pencil and a piece of paper. That's probably not too costly. However, to begin digital photography, you'll need a digital camera, a printer, software, and maybe a computer. That's a bit more of a consideration than a pencil and paper.

Your research should provide a *ballpark* figure for the potential start-up expenses and the cost to keep the activity going.

Your investigation will also tell you where to find the equipment you'll need. Sometimes this is obvious (if you want to paint or draw, you visit an art store); sometimes it's not (where do you go to buy a good marionette for your puppet show?).

Even when the sources are obvious, though, thorough research can offer you a wide range of available outlets. This wider selection, as a result of your research, often offers you better value and better quality.

4. To Acquire a Feel for the Level of Expertise You'll Need:

Stop into any bowling alley in the nation, observe briefly, and you'll see that you don't have to be an expert to enjoy the activity. The same applies to any creative activity you want to pursue. There's no obligation to become an expert in the field. If you enjoy writing, you don't have to rival Hemingway. If you'd like to present a bit of magic to your friends, you can certainly be less accomplished than Houdini. The fun is in the doing.

However, some may want to learn something about the quality that is necessary to become even competent or mediocre at an activity. Doing a bit of research can help you determine that.

5. To Obtain an Estimate of the Expense Required:

We've already touched on the cost of purchasing equipment, but there may be other costs connected with continuing certain activities—lessons, membership fees, additional supplies, who knows what all? Well, you'll know *what all* once you do the research. It's an important consideration.

6. To Discover Where and How You Can Learn More:

Each bit of knowledge you acquire leads to more knowledge that you want to acquire. The more you learn, the more you realize how much you don't know...but want to know. Good research not only informs you, but also leads you to other sources of even more information.

This pursuit of information can become a creative activity itself. The more involved you get in your project, the more you'll want to know about it. So, the pleasure is not only in the doing, but also in continuing to learn so much more about what it is you're doing.

7. To Discover Where and How You Can Find Qualified Instruction:

The pleasure does remain largely in the doing. And presumably, the better you perform, the more you'll enjoy it. You don't have to be an expert to enjoy your activity, but continuing to improve does enhance the enjoyment.

As you become more skilled in your activity, you'll need the guidance of those who are even more accomplished than you are in order to keep improving. Who are the qualified instructors and where can they be found? Your research will provide this information. Also, it will list schools, seminars, workshops, and organizations that can help in your continuing education.

The question now is: Where do you begin your research? The answer is: almost anywhere. It's an interesting phenomenon that beginning a research project is almost like hopping onto a merry-go-round—you can jump on anyplace and it will take you round and round. Each phase of your investigation not only provides facts, but also leads to sources of even more information. A listing on the Internet may lead to an interesting magazine article. The magazine piece may mention outstanding performers in the field. Contact with one of those experts could lead to conventions, schools, or seminars. And the merry-go-round continues on its way.

Following are several sources for research. You can attack them in sequence, out of sequence—all at once, or one at a time. The investigative process is one of exploration and following whichever way the clues lead.

a. The Internet:

The answer to almost anything you'd like to know about today is "Google it." Get onto the Internet, type in a few key words, and peruse the many suggestions it offers. If you find what you're looking for, fine. If you don't, you select different key words. With perseverance, the trial and error search should yield the answer to your questions. Or, it will suggest other areas to search.

You can also use specific websites on the Internet to help in your search. Amazon.com and Barnesandnoble.com list almost every book on every subject that is available. You can search by title, by subject matter, or by author and find some interesting reference material. Also, these sites often list magazines and periodicals, so you might be able to find one devoted to whichever activity you're investigating.

b. The Library:

If you don't trust your computing skills, or if you don't own a computer, you can resort to the traditional first stop in research— your local library. Go through the same trial and error method manually. Look up your key words to see if they reveal books or magazines related to your specific interest.

Don't neglect the librarian, either. Usually, librarians are interested in gathering information and are cooperative in either finding information for you or guiding you as you investigate on your own.

c. Specialized Newsletters and Magazines:

There is a magazine or newsletter devoted specifically to almost any activity or craft imaginable. There's a magazine called *Knitting* and one called *Crocheting*. There's a *Model Airplane News* and *Model Shipwright* for model enthusiasts.

The magazine devoted to the field you've chosen will feature informational articles about the craft, as well as instructional articles. It will most likely have ads relating to everything about the specific field—instruction, supplies, associations, seminars, and so on.

d. Individual Practitioners:

People who are interested in a particular field are usually interested in others who are interested in that same field. Contacting someone who is a recognized authority in the field—either by letter, e-mail, or phone call—gives him or her the opportunity to offer you a wide range of expertise and knowledge. They can recommend other places and other people where you can gain even more knowledge.

e. Manufacturers or Vendors:

Certainly the people that produce oil and watercolor paints want to see as many people as possible take an interest in art. They want you to know as much as possible about the craft and the paints, brushes, and other paraphernalia you would use. They want you to compare their products not only with competitors, but also with each other. Contacting them can bring you valuable information about their traditional products, along with information about new innovations. They'll send you catalogs of the various pigments that they offer. A recent visit to one art supply website told me about a new line of water-mixable oil colors. Another art supply website offered several pages of users' tips, listing innovative, creative ways of using their products for varying techniques.

And, of course, if you want to learn something about building a model airplane, visit a hobby shop. If you want to pick up some nice close-up illusions for your new interest, magic, ask the clerk at the magic supply outlet. These people know their wares and want to be as informative as possible. They want you to be interested in their materials and to be happy with whatever you purchase. They're eager to help you in order to help their repeat sales.

f. Clubs, Associations, and Organizations:

Just as there are specialized magazines devoted to almost every field, so there are groups of people interested in specific fields who form small clubs and national or international associations. People interested in writing can find a writer's club in practically any city or village in the country. These may only be a small group of people who meet periodically to read and critique each other's writing. People interested in public speaking or lecturing can join Toastmasters International, which has members all over the world. The organization is devoted to improving the speaking skills of all of its members. Belonging to similar organizations can offer valuable information about whichever activity you're pursuing.

Also, if there are no clubs or associations covering the pursuit you're interested in, why not organize one on your own? It only takes a few people who have similar interests to get a local club started. In this way, you can share your enthusiasm, critique one another's work, and learn from the experiences of your colleagues.

g. Conventions, Workshops, and Seminars:

Attending any one of these functions, whenever you can find them, is a valuable source of information. Not only do they offer classes, but you also gain information from a personal exchange with the accomplished lecturers, seminar leaders, and professionals who attend, and you also mingle and exchange information with peers—people like yourself who are interested in the subject and searching for information.

h. Fishing Expeditions:

Often you'll hear this term in connection with legal procedures. One lawyer might object that the opposing counsel is conducting a "fishing expedition." This means that they're searching for information without a solid basis in fact and without sufficient legal cause. Legally, this might be considered unethical, but when you're hunting for information, it's perfectly acceptable. If you have an avenue that *might* generate information, try it. If it might not generate results, try it anyway. Explore any paths you can and accept any information they might yield.

i. Anything Else You Can Think of:

This is not an exact science. It's pretty much a hit-and-miss endeavor. The items listed above are not the only means of gathering information.

If you can think of something else, give it a shot. It's the knowledge you gain that's important; not your method of producing it.

* * *

I've listed several reasons for and several methods of research in order to get your new creative activity started. Remember, though, that learning about your new craft is an ongoing process. You want to keep acquiring information through whatever means you can as you continue to practice your new skill. Know, too, that the experience you gain as you pursue this endeavor will yield knowledge of and by itself. Keep doing, keep learning, and keep enjoying.

This research helps you acquire the *intellectual knowledge* of your creative activity. Now let's get into the "Learning" phase of beginning this new creative project.

Chapter 14

Learning

It's nitty-gritty time. You've decided to do something creative. You've even decided which activity to pursue. You've done some research and know much more now about your activity than when you started. Possibly, the only thing you don't know now is *how to do it.*

You may think you know how to do it. You may read the recipe for a delicious pineapple meringue pie in a magazine. That magazine even features a picture that shows you how appetizing the finished product will look on your table. You mix the ingredients—heating, stirring, and folding when advised. Yet, you wind up with liquid filling rather than a nice custard to support the meringue. The only thing you can do with your resulting concoction is add vodka to it and serve it as a refreshing tropical drink.

I know how to play golf. Put a wooden tee in the ground, set the ball on it, swing hard at it, and knock the ball 270 yards down the fairway. I put the wooden stick in the ground, balance the ball on top of it, swing fiercely at it, and propel the ball 7 yards in front and to the right of me.

You don't yet *know how* to make a pineapple meringue pie and I don't yet *know how* to hit a golf ball.

The *knowing how* we're speaking of here is the actual hands-on, sweat of the brow, detailed, devoted labor that produces a satisfying result. It's more than knowing what to do; it's knowing how to do what we know how to do *competently.*

Where can we learn the skills we need?

There are many ways we can learn. Another cook may offer the solution to your soupy pineapple meringue pie. "Try adding corn starch to the recipe instead of flour. It works for me." In the case of my golf ineptitude, I might set up an appointment with a golf instructor to find out why my drives are falling 263 yards short of the 270 yards I'm entitled to.

Often the mode of education is dictated by the particular creative activity you've selected. Following are several suggestions for learning enough to get you started in whichever pursuit you've chosen. Determine which ones apply to your particular endeavor and go for it. Once you begin, you'll discover, too, that you learn as you go. You'll probably also learn that the more you learn, the more you'll want to learn.

1. Just Plunge In:

A youngster was telling his buddy about his favorite uncle, Uncle Philo. He was thrilled with a recent experience. "My Uncle Philo took me out in a rowboat to the middle of the lake and even though he knew that I didn't know how to swim, he tossed me into the water." "Wow," his friend said, "What did you do?" The youngster said, "I screamed and yelled for help, but Uncle Philo just watched me." "Wow," his friend said again. The boy said, "Then suddenly, I started to calm down. I started swimming." "Are you sure he wasn't trying to drown you?" the friend asked. The boy said, "No. Just by tossing me into the water, my uncle taught me to swim." His friend was impressed. "And guess what?" the boy added, "Tomorrow he's going to teach me how to fly."

Many people claim that the best way to learn to swim is to just plunge in. Perhaps putting your life in jeopardy is unwise, but just beginning your specific creative activity may be one way to learn it.

Writers always insist that the three best ways to learn how to write are to write, to write, and to write. If you're interested in pencil sketching, why not sharpen a pencil, get a piece of paper, and start drawing, drawing, and drawing?

Many activities lend themselves to *just doing it*. The doing is an educational process in itself. I guarantee that if I go out each day and hit 500 golf balls on the driving range, many of them will eventually go farther than my original 7-yard drive. Some of them may even be pretty good.

Initial efforts may not be polished or perfect, but they do begin the educational process.

Heck, your next pineapple meringue pie may be a culinary masterpiece.

2. Learn from a Friend:

Remember the excitement of finally reaching that age where you could apply for a learner's permit to drive a car? You were old enough to drive. However, you were frightened by the prospect, too. How do you turn the thing on? How do you shift into gear? How fast should you go? How do you stop this thing? It was all terrifying, but you wanted to drive. How could you risk going into traffic when you didn't know what to do once you were in traffic?

Chances are, despite a few driving schools and some driver education classes in school, you had a friend teach you. This good buddy sat next to you and told you step-by-step what to do. Insert the key in the ignition. Hold your foot on the brake as you release the parking brake. Keep your foot on the brake as you shift into "drive." Now ease your foot onto the accelerator.

You probably also learned how to tie the bait onto your fishing line from you dad or your cousin. You learned to make a batch of brownies under your mother's watchful guidance.

If you have a patient friend who knows the activity you'd like to learn and is willing to offer some instruction, take advantage of it.

3. Learn from Associations:

Have you ever watched a movie where a relaxed old farmer was sitting quietly on his porch with a chunk of wood in one hand and a knife in the other, calmly shaving away slivers of wood to form the piece of pine into a work of art? Well, for all you know, that gentleman may be the president of his local chapter of the NWCA—the National Woodcarvers Association. Yes, whittlers have a national organization.

Almost every activity you can imagine has a local, national, or international club for the enthusiasts. The purpose of these organizations is not only to benefit the individual practitioners, but also to promote and improve the image and quality of the craft. Often, they'll offer classes, seminars, or instruction in the activity because it benefits the individual practitioner while also benefiting the craft.

If you want to whittle, why not let a bunch of devoted whittlers teach you to whittle? As you learn to whittle, they may also help you find ways to promote and market your wares.

Whatever we said about whittling applies to whatever activity you've selected. Find an organization and take advantage of the educational services it offers.

4. Learn from Manufacturers or Vendors:

People who make computers wish that everyone in the world knew how to use a computer. Camera stores want everyone who passes by their window to know how to snap a picture. They both want you to learn more and more about their products because the more you know, the more you'll progress. Of course, the more you progress, the more equipment you'll need. If you become quite accomplished, you'll probably want or need the more expensive equipment. It's just good business. Consequently, manufacturers and vendors are inclined to offer you as much education as you'll need.

Most of this information is there simply for the asking. Tell a clerk in any camera store what you'd like to do, but don't know how to do, and he or she will volunteer a quick lesson in the use of the various photographic equipment they sell. If you don't get all the answers you want, ask more questions. They'll most likely be willing to furnish an answer or supply information that will help you find the answer.

Call the sales office of any computer or computer accessories manufacturer and ask questions. You'll probably receive a quick, on-the-phone beginner's course and an offer to receive pamphlets or instruction booklets that can be valuable learning tools.

For any activity that you select, you'll probably require some sort of materials. The people who make those materials and the people who sell them are valuable sources of education. Take advantage of it.

5. Learn from Classroom Instruction:

Sitting in a schoolroom with a notebook and textbook before you and a teacher lecturing at the front of the room is probably the most traditional and arguably the most effective learning procedure.

It's the only way to learn to become a doctor or a lawyer, and it may be the best way to learn to become anything else. I remember a comedian once who was playing the part of a doctor. He said, "I never really studied medicine, but I did hang around that doctor place—oh yeah, the hospital—for several weeks."

Probably the best way to learn anything is to *take a course* in it. But where?

Colleges: For some activities, a college degree might be useful. For instance, majoring in drama would be helpful to an aspiring actor. An English degree would certainly benefit a writer. However, many colleges offer specific classes. Some even offer a class in stand-up comedy. These classes may be offered by large or small universities, junior colleges, or community colleges. Several even offer free non-credit classes for people over a certain age.

With a bit of research, you should be able to find college instruction in your particular pursuit.

Adult Education Classes: Just about every city, town, village, region, or whatever offers some form of education for adults. The classes they offer can be quite eclectic, ranging from aerobic exercising to…well…maybe even whittling. I saw an item in the catalogue mailed to my house that taught "Sculpting a Portrait in Clay." I signed up. When I got to the school, I learned my daughter was taking a class in "Voice-over for Television." We both enjoyed the low pressure learning experience and came away knowing more than when we went in.

Associations: Often various organizations or clubs will offer classroom study in their particular field—even for non-members. What better way to learn a skill than from the people who have joined together to promote that skill?

Manufacturers and Vendors: Yes, we discussed them earlier. They will offer free advice over the telephone, in person, or via brochures and instructional booklets. However, many of them also offer formal classroom study. Computer stores, for example, often hold general classes in computer use, or they offer lessons in using the various software packages that they sell. It's worth a phone call to the sales department or to individual stores to ask about a curriculum.

6. Learn from Internet Classes, E-mail Courses, and Correspondence Courses:

All of us in the fifty-and-over age group have stories to tell that begin with, "It wasn't so easy back in the days when I went to school…" We continue with exaggerations like, "I had to walk three miles through the snow, through driving rains, through hurricanes…" and whatever else our imaginations could dream up. Now those complaints are passing into folklore. Today, the schools come to us.

Today you can attend class in your pajamas. Just switch on your computer and enroll in an online class. They come in all forms and formats. With many, you can actually have online classroom discussions with other students and receive instant feedback from your instructor. With others, you might simply "listen" to the lesson and then do whatever exercises are assigned.

The best way to find online classes offered for your particular interest is to search for it. Where else? Online.

There are also many courses offered as a variation of the traditional correspondence courses. They've eliminated the drudgery of licking envelopes, attaching postage, and dropping homework into the mailbox. All of the communication is done via e-mail. Again, there are many varying formats, but basically, you receive your lectures or lessons on your computer via an e-mail message, and you reply the same way.

Then there is the old stand-by correspondence course. Here, you receive your text material and your assignments through the mail. You study, do your homework, and hand in your assignments through the mail. This system is slower than the e-mail version, but that may be a blessing. It allows you time to concentrate on your reading and study while you're waiting for the instructor's response.

7. Learn from Trade Shows, Conventions, and Seminars:

Many of these get-togethers offer classroom instruction. Trade shows, of course, usually feature a large auditorium filled with booths of vendors and manufacturers displaying their standard wares and their latest innovations. However, there are also often side rooms offering instruction on various facets of whichever trade they're promoting. At publisher's trade shows, for example, you'll be able to wander around the trade floor and see the latest titles the publishers have available. You may also be able to find a class on "How to Approach an Agent with your Manuscript" or "Secrets of Writing Great Mystery Novels."

Conventions and seminars offer the same opportunity for classroom instruction.

8. Learn from Experts in the Field:

Years ago, when I worked for an electrical manufacturing firm, I had an assignment to organize engineering information into a logical format to be loaded into a computer program. I interviewed many of the engineers to learn what information they had. Most of them were reluctant to discuss the subject since they felt that the engineering logic was too diversified to ever be reduced to simple computer logic. I agreed with them, but asked, "If your superiors ordered you to categorize your information, where would you begin?"

Then they spoke freely. They told me what they knew.

Experts are usually glad to share their knowledge and skills with people who are genuinely interested in their art or craft. If you approach them politely, respecting the demands on their time, you'll often find that they're happy to supply information or suggest places where you can get the information.

This might simply be a letter (or an e-mail) or a phone call. Remember, though, the expert has no obligation to educate you. If you get a response, be grateful. If you get no response, simply move on to the next attempt.

Some may offer the advice freely, others may charge a fee for their assistance. Either way, any information you can collect from a polished practitioner is valuable.

Bob Hope told me a story once that relates to this concept. He had played in a golf exhibition with the great golfer, Ben Hogan. He asked if Hogan would give him a golf lesson. Hogan agreed. He told Hope, "Be on the driving range tomorrow morning at 8 o'clock." Bob Hope said, "Oh, I never get up that early in the morning." Hogan said, "Then you don't want a lesson from me."

Hope told me he showed up at 8 A.M.

All of the above suggestions imply that you are learning from someone who already knows the skill and is formally passing that information on to you, the student. However, you may be more inclined to teach yourself a new skill. Following are several ideas to help you accomplish your own self-training:

9. Learn from Kits or Materials:

Do you know how to build an Adirondack chair? Probably not. You'll learn in a hurry though if you order an Adirondack chair from a mail-order catalog and the box arrives marked, "Some Assembly Required." That's right. You haven't purchased an Adirondack chair; you've bought a bunch of parts that have to be put together to form an Adirondack chair.

But if you don't know how to build an Adirondack chair, how are you going to put it together? Somewhere in that collection of lumber, nuts, and bolts is a sheet or a booklet that tells you, step-by-step, *how to build* an Adirondack chair.

Many of the creative activities you might choose lend themselves to learning from the instructions included in the box. If you want to learn how to build a model airplane, for example, buy a model airplane kit and follow the instructions religiously from point one through to point 274.

By your third, or fifth, or tenth kit, you should be a pretty accomplished model airplane builder.

10. Learn from Books:

There's a saying, "Whatever's worth doing is worth doing well." There should also be one that says, "Whatever's worth doing is worth writing a book on how to do it." There are "how-to" books on whittling, reading music, cross-stitching. No matter what it is that you want to do, it's almost certain that someone has written a book telling you "how-to" do it. As noted previously, there are even "how-to" books on how to write "how-to" books.

Visit a library, a bookstore, or check book sellers' lists on the Internet and you'll surely find several volumes on whichever creative activity you want to pursue.

11. Learn from Videotapes or DVDs:

One advantage that these tools have over textbooks is that you can actually see the process evolving. For instance, in sculpting, a book may show a series of steps to form and shape the lips on a portrait. That's accurate and helpful. However, to see the artist lay the clay on and then take a specific tool and manipulate the material until it begins to look like a pair of lips is not only helpful, but also inspiring. You see it happen, you realize how it happened, and you begin to feel that if you use the same technique, you can make it happen, too.

The visual impact makes the lesson much more powerful. You've seen those artists on television who teach you with a few simple strokes how to paint a peaceful landscape or gorgeous flowers. They make it look so easy that you feel you can pick up a brush and do the same.

Often with practice, you can.

12. Learn from Example:

As a comedy writing teacher, I would tell the aspiring writers that the best instructor they could wish for was in the corner of their living room or den. It was the television set. If they wanted to learn to write situation comedies, they should watch the sitcoms that were on the air each week. If they paid attention to the style, the format, the dialogue, they could then replicate it by using their own imaginative writing.

If they wanted to write stand-up material for comedians, they should watch the comedians who were doing their acts on television. That would teach them about subject matter and how it's delivered. That's an education in writing stand-up material.

When I decided that I wanted to write comedy, I taped all of Bob Hope's television monologues, typed them out and studied them, then a few weeks later, I would pick new topics and try to write jokes about them in Bob Hope's style. This was my *formal* training in writing comedy.

Several years later, after I had achieved some success as a writer, Bob Hope called me and asked me to write material for his appearance on the Academy Awards broadcast. I wrote and submitted my gags. Hope used a few of them during his opening monologue as emcee of the Oscars.

He called the next day and said, "I liked your jokes. It looks like you've been writing for me all your life." I said, "Mr. Hope, I have, only you didn't know about it."

So, watch people who are already doing well at whatever it is you want to do. Emulate them, and you're getting a fine education.

13. Learn from Experience:

Sometimes my wife knits while we watch TV in the evening. Often I'll glance over and see her not knitting, but pulling apart what she has already knitted.

"Not going well?" I ask.

She'll say, "No, this thing wasn't working out the way I wanted."

But she's not upset. She simply says, "I think I found out what I was doing wrong, so I'll start over."

Writers, as I've mentioned, maintain that the three best ways to learn to write are to write, to write, and to write. With almost any activity we learn as we do.

It's not really automatic, though. One participant in a series of tennis lessons complained to the professional instructor, "I don't know what it is. I've got ten years of tennis experience and I don't ever seem to get any better."

The pro corrected him. He said, "You don't have ten years of experience. You have one year of experience ten times."

We do have to make a conscious effort to learn as we gain experience.

Chapter 15

Have Fun With It

Years ago I worked for a head comedy writer who would call the various staff writers with the day's writing assignments. He would list the several topics that we were to work on and invariably end with a negative admonition: "If you can find anything funny in these topics, you deserve a medal," "I guarantee there's not one good joke in this whole batch of topics," or "Good luck trying to find something funny in this pile of garbage."

What a black cloud to hang over the beginning of one's joke writing day.

When I became a head writer who had to hand out assignments, I would end each phone call with, "Have fun with it." I discovered that the writing would not only be easier when attacked with pleasant anticipation, but that it would be written more quickly and produce better results.

You've dutifully read through this book, selected one or several creative activities, done some research, gathered materials, taken a few classes, lessons, or taught yourself the basics. Now you're about to have some fun in whichever field you've chosen.

That's the key. It's not the end product. Sure, you want your work to turn out well, but if it doesn't, as we said, you can burn it, break it apart, bury it, or blow it up and start over again. If you had fun doing it, who cares?

Remember the wise words of Charles Schulz to those who felt that their efforts would never prove successful? He told them, "The reward is in the doing."

So get cranking on your project. Give it all the devotion and skill you have in you. Most of all, though, *have fun with it.*

Index

About the Author

Gene Perret began his TV writing career on the staff of *The Jim Nabors Hour*. He has served on the writing staffs of *Laugh-In, The Carol Burnett Show,* and *Mama's Family,* among others. He was head writer and producer for *Welcome Back, Kotter,* and *The Tim Conway Show.*

Perret also wrote for Bob Hope's special appearances and television specials from 1969 until Hope's retirement from show business. He traveled with all of the Hope USO shows, beginning in 1983, and served as Hope's head comedy writer for the last twelve years of the comedian's career.

Round Table is a newsletter that Gene Perret founded for people who are interested in comedy writing and performing. It's a place where comedy professionals—at all levels—can gather to share ideas, know-how, and laughs.

You can be a part of the *Round Table*. For more information, visit writingcomedy.com or contact *Round Table* at: Round Table, P.O. Box 786, Agoura Hills, CA, 91376, or call 818- 865-7833.

Gene also teaches e-mail courses on comedy writing and writing humorous articles for magazines. These are limited classes, with Gene providing personal feedback. For a class schedule or for more information contact us through the website at writingcomedy.com.